LEST WE FORGET

The Experiences of World War II
Westindian Ex-Service Personnel

by Robert N Murray

Edited by Patrick L Hylton

**NOTTINGHAM WESTINDIAN COMBINED
EX-SERVICES ASSOCIATION**

in association with Hansib Publishing (Caribbean) Limited

Supported by Nottinghamshire County Council

First published in 1996
Published by the Nottinghamshire Westindian Combined Ex-Services
Association, 28 Beaconsfield Street, Hyson Green, Nottingham NG7 6FD

Printed by Martins the Printers Ltd., Berwick upon Tweed

British Library Cataloguing-In-Publication Data.
A catalogue record for this book is available from the British Library.

ISBN 1-870518-52-7

DEDICATION TO VINCENT MILLER AND OTHERS

So Vin is gone! But Vin is not dead. As one colleague said, "Vin is not dead: he's here amongst us in spirit, if not in body. His memory will live on and on forever."

Very few who met Vin ever forgot him. To his Association colleagues he was one of the best. For him no task seemed too great to tackle, particularly in the interest of Nottingham Westindian Combined Ex-Services Association.

He was an Association man. He ate, drank and lived for the Association. Of him it could truly be said: "He worked tirelessly at times, above and beyond the call of duty, and we must never let his memory die."

FROM THE LORD MAYOR OF NOTTINGHAM

MR CHAIRMAN, Lord Lieutenant, Civic dignitaries, ladies and gentlemen.

On behalf of all your guests here today, Mr Chairman, I thank you for inviting us to join you and for your very warm welcome.

It has been a privilege to represent the City of Nottingham at your service today.

In March at the Elderly Voices Conference, Eric Irons gave a very moving description of how a Jamaican worker started a fund to provide a squadron to fight for Britain when this country was on its knees. I was ashamed and shocked that until then I had never heard of this squadron. I knew that the Westindies had provided troops but although I had read stories of the French Resistance, the Italian, Yugoslavian and Greek partisans and had seen cemeteries in France to the Africans and Indians who had fought in the First World War and even the history of those Germans who had fought facism, I had never read a word about the part the Westindians played. I knew that there had been soldiers from all over the Commonwealth and what was then the Empire, but that was all.

It is ironic that the Westindies helped this country tremendously during its hour of need and not ten years afterwards it was necessary to set up the Race Equality Council; so that just after fighting for freedom we had an organisation to fight for equality.

It is importnat for our children to know and have pride in their own culture. It is just as important that our children understand and respect people with different histories in our community.

To hate anyone because of their religion, colour or nationality is a canker in our society which we must unite and fight together. I hope this book will play a major part in that fight.

Speech by His Right Worshipful, The Lord Mayor of Nottingham, Councillor Sylvia Parsons to Civic dignitaries and other distinguished guests on the occasion of the 50th Anniversary of Victory in Europe Day, 13th May, 1995, at the AIFF Centre, Hysson Green, Nottingham

CONTENTS

FOREWORD

THE TWO WORLDS WARS in which Europe predominantly was involved unfortunately embodied Asia, Africa, Australia, New Zealand, the United States of America, Canada and more incredibly, the Westindies. Perhaps some understanding will be arrived at if we are aware of the fact that the Westindies were at the time of these hostilities historically known as the British Westindies. Hence our direct involvement in what was a European catastrophe. Westindians, because of their allegiance and loyalty to the crown, felt duty-bound to volunteer their services when Great Britain, acknowledged by and large as the Mother Country, came into direct conflict with the tyranny of Adolph Hitler's Nazi Germany.

Westindians from all walks of life enlisted for service in the Military Forces, in the Army, Air Force, the Fleet Air Arm, the Navy, the ATS, WAACS, and more so a great number of them civilians, went into ammunition factories and timber yards.

Many of these volunteers were mere teenagers but this did not deter them, and it is well known that many of them indulged in forgery in order to fit into the age criteria. Some volunteers even incurred the wrath of their parents or guardians because it was inconceivable for them to accept that their sons or daughters, just out of school, should leave their homes to travel thousands of miles to get involved in a war that was not their concern, and with the great possibility that they would be killed and would therefore not be seen again. It was also envisaged that because of the ties that may be established, many of these servicemen and servicewomen would no doubt remain in Europe.

This is one of the main reasons for the publication of this book. The men and women who left their homelands, leaving behind mothers, fathers, relatives, friends and, more importantly, their culture, and chose for many different reasons to fulfil their perceived obligations had no reason to think that the people of Great Britain, both at political and at grass roots level would forget the sacrifices made in order to respond to pleas for moral, physical and financial support from the Mother Country.

Despite these years of selfless sacrifice of thousands of men and women, the War Department have on numerous occasions claimed that there is no record available of the number of men and women from the Westindies and colonies involved in these two World Wars, but it is estimated that between 150,000 and 180,000 men and women enlisted for the Second World War.

We hope that this book will enlighten the reader of the difficult, insulting and sometimes nearly unbelievable circumstances encountered by those volunteers who chose to remain in Britain at the end of hostilities not realising that their attempt to settle and assimilate themselves into society would, through the short memories of the host population, not be acceptable.

Many of them are now retired, many are immobile and yet many more have departed this life. We salute these stalwarts, and so we should, for these are the men and women who helped to preserve our liberty and democratic way of life. These unsung heroes have until now been excluded from the local and national history. This book will we believe, make an important contribution to correcting this unfortunate omission.

Herman Deane
June , 1995

ACKNOWLEDGEMENTS

The Nottingham Westindian Combined Ex-Services Association wishes to thank a number of individuals and institutions for contributions to this book, they include:

Herman Deane in respect of the sterling work performed by him. He extended his talents to several aspects of the book including the compilation of the material in the early stage, spending a great deal of time in doing so.

Len Garrison Director of the Association of Caribbean Families (ACFF) Education and Cultural Centre and consultant to this publishing project. He gave the benefit of his historical studies, research and publishing experience by way of ideas, advice and guidance.

Harry Joshua, for the highly professional work done as coordinator of the project in it's early phases, he also contributed much expertise in documenting the oral histories of the Ex-Servicemen and women.

Jean Lewis for her commitment and dedication shown whilst transcribing the oral accounts, using her linguistic skills to translate some interviews from Jamaican vernacular into standard English. Hers was a most invaluable contribution.

David H Lewis for his weekly visits to our Association office, assisting the progression of this long overdue publication.

Dr Hugh Miller of Nottingham Trent University for his valuable comments in respect of an earlier draft. Also to the Nottingham Trent University for contribution of reproductory resources without which progress on this book would have been severely hampered.

The Nottinghamshire County Council for not only imparting moral support, but contributing substantially to the funding of this publication project, without which, this book would not have become a reality.

Arif Ali and his team at *Caribbean Times.*

A special thank you is equally due to the following persons, whose praises have remained largely unsung until now, fifty years on; they are:

Esther Armagon
Gerald Beard
Mrs Norma Best
Carl Brewster
Carol Campbell
Ulric Cross
Tony Daley
Ivor De'Souza
Ronald Hall
George Haynes
Bill Henriques
Stanley Hodges
Brewster A Holder
Frank Holder
Eric Hudson
Vernon Hunte
Pasteur Irons
Alfred Keith Levy
Oliver Marshall
Sidney Mathews

James Mckenzie
Dudley Miller
Vincent Miller
James Moore
Robert Murray
Adrian Neysnich
Godfrey Petgrave
Laurie Phillpotts
Alwyn Pindar
George Powe
Mrs Muriel Reader *(James Moore's daughter)*
Bob Roach
Gerry Smith
Billy Strachan
Owen Sylvester
Dudley Thompson
Arthur Wint

WHO'S WHO?
Contributors to this book

ESTHER ARMAGON - ATS served from 1944 in UK. Midwife after War.

GERALD BEARD - Joined RAF in 1943. Successfully defended by Norman Manley - eminent Jamaican K C while in the service.

NORMA BEST - ATS served from 1944 in UK. Headmistress after War.

CARL BREWSTER - Served in RAF from June 1944. Chiropodist after War.

CAROL CAMPBELL - Made own way to England. Joined ATS.

ULRIC CROSS - Squadron leader - DSO/DFC and highest ranking Westindian airman in World War II. Became High Court Judge in Westindies. Later became High Commissioner for Trinidad and Tobago in England.

TONY DALEY - RAF from 1944.

IVOR DE'SOUZA - Served in RAF from 1940 - Flight Lieutenant - Flight Commander to Australian Squadron.

RONALD HALL - Joined RAF in 1940. Passed out as Sergeant. Fought in Italy. Rise in rank became meteoric after it became known he spoke French and Italian fluently.

GEORGE HAYNES - Joined RAF in 1944. After initial training transferred to RAF regiment till end of War.

STANLEY HODGES - Joined RAF in 1944.

BREWSTER AHLESTON HOLDER - Joined RAF in 1944.

ERIC HUDSON - Joined RAF in 1944.

FRANK HOLDER - RAF in 1944. Boxer, athlete and singer of some repute. In 1956 voted top male vocalist by *Melody Maker*.

PASTEUR IRONS - Among the first ground - crew to join RAF in 1943. Welcomed by the Colonial Secretary, Sir Oliver Stanley at Liverpool before going on to Filey, Yorkshire.

SIDNEY MATHEWS - RAF 1944-49

JAMES MCKENZIE - Joined RAF in 1944. Spent many years in England before returning to Jamaica in 1991.

ROBERT MURRAY - Joined RAF in 1944. Became educational instructor towards the end of the War.

VINCENT MILLER - Joined RAF in 1944. Largely responsible for recording of the Jamaica Interviews.

GODFREY PETGRAVE - Father Jamaican, mother Antiguan. Father working in Nigeria at outbreak of war. Joined RAF in Lagos, August 1943. Became chiropodist after the War.

LAURIE PHILLPOTTS - RAF. Arrived in England early 1944. Another who was welcomed by the Colonial Secretary, Sir Oliver Stanley. Attached to Aircrew for different operations as teleprinter/operator.

ALWYN PINDAR - Joined RAF in 1944. Wanted an occupation in upholstering after War, but ended up a taxi driver.

GEORGE POWE - Joined RAF in 1943. Wireless operator. Made sizeable contribution to this book.

BILLY STRACHAN - Left Jamaica at the age of 18, paying his own fare - arriving in England with £3.00 in his pocket, knowing no one. He joined the RAF as a wireless Operator/Airgunner, passing out as a sergeant, later becoming a pilot-officer, flying Wellington bombers and engaging in many daring raids over Germany.

ARTHUR WINT - One of the outstanding Westindian airmen of the Second World War. A brilliant athlete who won a gold medal in the 440 yards, representing his native country - Jamaica - in the 1948 Olympics. He was also High Commissioner to the UK between July 1974 and March 1978. After leaving the RAF he studied medicine, becoming Dr Arthur Wint.

INTRODUCTION

"I'm speaking to you from the Cabinet Room of No. 10 Downing Street. This morning the British Ambassador in Germany handed the German Government a note stating that, unless they withdrew their troops from Poland by 11.00am a state of war exists between us. I have to tell you now that no such undertaking was received and, consequently, this country is at war with Germany."

When, on 3rd September, 1939, Sir Neville Chamberlain, Prime Minister of England, in slow, measured tones, uttered those now memorable words, most of the contributors to this book were in their teens, some in their early teens. Robert Murray remembers the broadcast as vividly as if made yesterday. He had left school at 16, put to several trades by his father who, realising that his son had no future at working with his hands, had sent him back to school - high school - for him to try and distinguish himself in the academic field. It was while sitting on his front steps, studying English History (1066-1487) for his Junior Cambridge Examination, that young Robert heard the broadcast on a neighbour's radio. From that moment, he recalls, pandemonium ensued. There were not many cars then but, in Georgetown, capital of British Guiana, now Guyana, hundreds of bells - bicycle bells, church bells and every other bell available - rang out to spread the news. Men, as usual on these occasions, were rushing to the Cable and Wireless Board to read the war proclamation for themselves. Immediately the entire Caribbean area - exceedingly patriotic at the time - indicated their desire to help. Trinidad and Tobago, Barbados and Jamaica and indeed, Guyana, pledged their urgent support to the "Mother Country". In addition, Jamaica forthwith promised a squadron of spitfires - later to be known as the Jamaican Squadron - and Barbados, regarded as Little England, encouraged:

"Go ahead Big England, Little England is behind you."

From then on there followed a stream of enquiries from ordinary men and women throughout the Caribbean volunteering to help, and they did help from the earliest days of the War to the very end ; Westindians, men and women, played their part in the British Forces - in the Army, the Royal Air Force, the Royal Navy, the Merchant Navy, as nurses in the hospitals, and in welfare and voluntary services and munition factories. Yet the story of the contribution made by Westindians, men and women, during two World Wars - but particularly World War Two - has never been told.

Similarly, the experiences of ex-service personnel as pathfinders in the modern phase of post-War Westindian immigration has only been incidentally explored. Both of these stories are important in their own right. Telling the story of the contribution made during World War Two is important because:-

(a) It is part of the heritage of the wider community and of Westindian peoples in particular.

(b) It will bring to light, possibly for the first time, the unique experiences of Westindians serving in the Armed Forces during the War, and;

(c) It will directly counter that popular but mistaken assertion that the Westindian community, while benefiting from Britain's post-War economic boom, sacrificed little or nothing during the War itself.

Examining the pathfinding role of ex-service personnel in immigration is important because:-

I. Though race relations have led to intensive study of the second generation and, to a lesser extent, of the first, the crucial role played in the early settlement process by resettled black ex-service personnel remains largely unexamined.

II. There are many children and grandchildren of Westindian ex-service personnel who, apart from vague references to service in some part of the British forces during the last War, have seen no tangible evidence, documentary or otherwise, that their parents, grandparents or distant relatives played any part whatsoever. Neither do many in the host community have the foggiest idea that Westindians amongst them contributed in any way towards the War victory.

The aims and objectives of this book, therefore, are to put the record straight and in so doing:

1. To highlight some of the contributions made by Westindians, predominantly from the Nottingham and Derby areas of England, whilst acknowledging that the circumstances could very well apply to any Westindian who served in the UK during the last War wherever he or she might be at present.

2. To portray through oral histories the war experiences and settlement afterwards in the UK of many of these Westindian people - the vast majority of whom were recruited in the Westindies in 1943/44 to replace those British members of the Royal Air Force groundcrews who were needed elsewhere - particularly in the Middle East. Records show that individuals and small batches of Westindians played their part in various branches of the British Armed Forces from the very outbreak of hostilities, some arriving in the United Kingdom as early as 1940.

Three substantial groups of Westindian recruits reached England in 1944, and one arrived early in 1945. Other groups were being recruited and trained when the War ended, rendering further departures for the UK unnecessary.

Lest We Forget, for the most part, has been written from the perspective of those Westindian RAF ground-crew personnel who made up the fourth and final group. This was, perhaps, the largest group and differed slightly in certain aspects (e.g. places of arrival in the UK, manner of reception on arrival and internecine strife amongst the recruits - albeit briefly) from the three previous groups. It is, however, hoped that the contents of this book will be seen to be representative of the experiences of most Westindians who served in the UK during World War Two and will not detract from its aims and objectives.

Robert N. Murray

17

PRE-RECRUITMENT

The war against Nazi Germany's aspirations was not only fought by, nor did it only affect, those whose homelands were immediately under threat; it also had an impact on those from further afield. What had started as a European conflict escalated into a World conflagration involving Britain, who still retained colonial rule over a vast empire, including the Caribbean. The experiences of the ex-service personnel from the various Caribbean Islands, recalling their sense of attachment to, and kinsmanship with Britain as their "Motherland", made the War seem more immediate to them. Many still remember the high esteem in which Britain was held. One ex-serviceman explains:

> "I held England in very great esteem. I read every book about England I could lay my hands on. I knew almost everything about England, every coalfield and every steel-work, their size and disposition. All our geography in school was based entirely on England. Whilst one knew very little about Westindian history, one's brain was full of knowledge where English history was concerned. We were always told - and we always had this thing at the back of our minds - that England was the Mother Country. So we held her in the highest regard and this was shown in patriotism."

Ulric Cross, a Trinidadian, reveals in the comment below the intense interest in Britain that existed in the Caribbean:

> "To some extent I was not entirely unfamiliar with England, although I had never been to the country. My uncle was a doctor in Bolton, Lancashire ...... ever since I was a child ..... *The Overseas Daily Mirror, London Illustrative News, The Trailer*, a number of English magazines, we got regularly every month from him. One got, through these magazines, a very good insight into a cross-section of English life. We also knew quite a lot about the English at school. I knew more about the history of England than the history of the Westindies when I was at school."

Adrian Neysnich, a Jamaican, typifies the sense of being a part of Britain that was prevalent in the Caribbean, and hence involvement with a war in another sphere of the world, when he says:

> "We were under British control, as is known. We were all from the Westindies which was under British rule. Since Great Britain was in a war I felt like it was my duty to take part in helping to gain victory for Her, for ourselves and for the world."

Billy Strachan, also from Jamaica, was born in 1921 - a lively boy for whom adventure mirrored the epitome of life. He went to the famous Woolmer's School and Alma Mater of many a Jamaican athlete, leaving in December 1939 - just four months after the war began. From that moment Billy had only one thing on his mind - to get to England and become involved in helping the "Mother Country" - by being involved in hostilities. He intended leaving for the UK as soon as the opportunity presented itself.

"I never thought of the Army or Navy. The next adventure on my list was to fly aeroplanes. And there were none in Jamaica."

Hence, for most servicemen irrespective of which Islands in the Caribbean they hailed from, a sense of attachment was felt towards Britain. Individuals who took an opposite view to this sense of patriotism and of being a part of Britain faced scorn, ridicule or worse, as the following story told by another fellow before his recruitment, instances:

> "There was a Portuguese man who was a linesman on the railway. He was always praising Hitler and Mussolini until one night my father lost his temper and hit him. He then called the police and had him arrested for treason. That's how patriotic we were."

This feeling of allegiance and being part of Britain was reflected to a great extent in the coverage the local media gave the War. Stanley Hodges from Jamaica recalls information on the War being given through the *Daily Gleaner* and radio. Robert Murray recalls this information as being extensive, in that:

> "The newspapers were full of it every day, and there were always arguments for and against. Television did not exist in those days, of course, but the radio station carried regular news and the latest headlines. I remember going down to the Cable and Wireless Board to read the latest bulletins."

However, Westindian service personnel were soon to recognise that colonization was not the same as acceptance by the British. James Moore, a Jamaican who had also fought in the First World War, was living in Nottingham, England, at the outbreak of the Second World War. His experiences and those of his family bring into sharp focus the contradiction between what black people were being told in the Caribbean about Britain being their Motherland and the actual perception that existed of black people who were living in Britain. His daughter, Muriel Reader, recalls how they were made aware of not being accepted, being different and being viewed as aliens:

"I remember we were conscious of it because nowhere we looked could we find anyone who liked us. Wherever we went we were regarded as little freaks, someone always wanted to touch us, take a little piece of our hair or something like that."

The immediacy of the War in the Caribbean was further accentuated by regular nightly blackouts, the local army being on constant alert. The effect of hostilities on supplies was taking its toll and the proximity of some aspects of the War showed signs of causing some anxiety. The Battle of the River Plate was one such instance. This battle took place just off the coast of Guyana between two British frigates and a German battleship in which, rather than surrender, the Germans scuttled their ship. The memory of this battle lingers to this day. One person, a mere boy at the time, recalls how this battle had captured the attention of people living in the immediate area and beyond.

"For days afterwards the newspapers were full of stories and vivid pictures of the battle .... people couldn't stop talking about this piece of the War on their own doorsteps ....Being young, I was most impressed to learn how this great German battleship, I believe it was called the *Graaf Spe*, was sighted, pursued and trapped by two tiny British frigates."

With the Caribbean Islands being dependent on imported goods during the War, shortages were experienced by some individuals. Stanley Hodges, "to his knowledge," did not recall any shortages of goods in Jamaica as a direct result of the War, stating that any shortages might have been due to a hurricane which had occurred recently. However, a Guyanese ex-serviceman did recall shortages of food in his country:

> "My father being a baker, the shortage of flour affected his business considerably. I recall serving in the shop when a few little bags of flour came in and pandemonium started. Men and women would be scrambling and screaming for bread. Of course, many had to go without. They then had to turn to baking their own bread from cassava flour - not a very good substitute, but then there were shortages of all the other imported products, which were many."

Athleston Holder would never forget how some individuals capitalized on the scarcity of goods:

> "Yes, it affected us in terms of food because Jamaica during that period imported over 55% of its food, a lot of which could not enter the Island because of the War. There were all sorts of shortages imaginable, and a lot of hoarding took place. If you found anybody that had the kind of food we liked, he or she became a little God in the community."

In Britain, James Moore and his family were facing hardship even before the Second World War had begun, both from racism and the economic situation at the time. His daughter remembers their being "poorer than poor," and recalls one incident that typified their plight in Nottingham:

> "..... before the War my father used to work for a man, Mr Fox, on Derby Road. Mr Fox had a shop there. My father did some work for him and this man was supposed to pay him for the job. My father had worked for Mr Fox before and we were desperate. My father did not have any money and he had no idea where the next meal was coming from. After completing the job, the man refused to pay my father who had been running backwards and forwards for his little pay without success. So, to satisfy himself and to feed his children, my father took some saws that were hanging in Mr Fox's shop and pawned them. The little money he came back with, he spent on food for us - his wife and children. I remember coming home from school at lunch-time, and seeing two men in the house. Somehow we recognised them as detectives. The next thing I knew was that they took my father away and my mother was crying .... I think they kept him that night and let him out the next morning, I don't remember whether they fined him or not. But this is

22

just to show the meanness of that man and the injustices that existed."

With the allegiance of Westindians, the scant availability of goods and the paucity of employment at that period, a rich and fertile source of recruitment into the British Forces was available in the Westindies. Advertisements for potential draftees into the Royal Air Force drew volunteers from a variety of backgrounds and for reasons that were not always confined to patriotism, as will be seen later. Meanwhile James Moore had been seeking work - any kind of work he could get and a chance to fulfil his ambitions. This was not to be. He found very few openings in his line of work at that time, and had to 'eke out' an existence by indulging in casual labour and, on very few occasions, working as a film extra if he was fortunate. According to his daughter, it was whilst engaged as a film extra that he met Paul Robeson, a leading Black concert singer and actor of the day. James Moore had intended to work alongside Paul Robeson in a film called 'Valley of the River', but, as his daughter recalls, this aspiration never materialised. Any kind of work failed to become a possibility:

> "....... (he) just couldn't get a job until the War came and that was the reason he went in .... to get support for us. He joined the army as soon as the War started. It may have been about two days after, he came home and said he was going in the army."

Gerald Beard, living in Portland, Jamaica, was working with his father as a carpenter. He had intended to take up his father's trade. However, his father became ill and was not available to him. On hearing about the RAF recruitment he decided to join up:

> "I was not all that much interested until one of my friends said to me, 'Why not join up! Join along with me?' He was a very good friend, so I thought I'll do it .... (but also) .... when we were in Jamaica we thought that Britain was the Motherland, so I thought I would be doing a good service in that respect."

Stanley Hodges, who was from Kensington, Jamaica, and whose parents were small farmers, originally took up employment as a cabinet-maker under the guidance of a handyman introduced to him by his father. After working with this handyman for a year he

23

realised that he wasn't "learning anything", and observed that:

> "Westindians were invited to volunteer for the army and the RAF. My life then seemed to be at a standstill, and when I thought of the possibility of coming to England, the Motherland as we knew it then, I decided to volunteer for the RAF."

Even those who had good employment viewed the opportunity of going to Britain as attractive. Robert Murray, who had followed an academic career and was in a good occupation, felt compelled to join the RAF as a means to an end:

> "Even though I had a good job, I could not see myself getting terribly far in the firm. Somehow I did not rate my chances very highly. I felt that I would always remain at the bottom even though, on the point of leaving, the boss tried to persuade me to stay. He said: "Don't go. These people here are all getting older and there is time for you to rise. You could become an accountant, because we're an up-and-coming firm." But nothing he said could have changed my mind. I was hell-bent on going. Another reason was that I was young and adventurous and the thought of joining the Royal Air Force and serving in England fired my imagination. I'd read a lot about England, in some ways I knew more about it than my own country. Now I was going there. Snowballs in hell could not stop me now."

James Mckenzie and George Powe are both Jamaicans. James Mckenzie was assisting his father in agriculture, and George Powe's parents were grocers while he attended college (the equivalent of High School). For Ulric Cross the prospect of entering the RAF was an opportunity to fulfil a lifelong ambition.

> "....... I used to read a lot of flying stories before the War. I was very interested in aeroplanes and there was a war going on."

The Nazis were far from inactive in response to the British recruitment drive. They transmitted propaganda in an attempt to stem the influx of Westindian people recruited into the British Forces and this generated heated debate within the community. George Powe recalls:

24

"...... the Germans used to broadcast a lot of propaganda to Jamaica and told us things like the British are only using the black people. It was discussed all over Kingston. Every corner you went people would discuss and talk about the War and many people said that they would not fight for Britain because Britain had enslaved us for a number of years and so on."

Again, individuals who were seen to take an opposite view to that which supported Britain faced sanctions, ridicule and sometimes ostracism. George Powe articulates an exemplar incident concerning this censorship by stating:

"There was a writer called Roger Mais who published an article entitled, 'Now we Know'; He was arrested because the article depicted British Imperialism in its naked form and .... explained to the people why they should not fight for Britain. He quoted the experience of the Emperor Haile Selassie and the Italian intervention in Africa. Many people were concerned about this and said that we should not fight."

In response the British government adopted counter-propaganda strategies in an attempt to suppress the rise of dissenting voices. He remembers the use of fear tactics:

"..... and that it was a good thing to help the Motherland because if we didn't, we would be enslaved by the conquerors, that is the Nazis, the Italians and so on."

In the event, George Powe acknowledged all these arguments but:

"I knew all this, but in spite of this I came because my friends were coming."

Athleston Holder also enlisted in the Forces because of peer influence. He was living with his grandparents and heard about the British recruitment from friends in Montego Bay, Jamaica. Therefore, he decided to follow the example of his contemporaries and enlisted.

The possibility of a better life was also an inducement for individuals to enter the military. The perception of Britain as a prosperous country fostered this belief, causing one recruit to observe:

"I also had this feeling that I could better myself in England - although I did not know how or why. I told myself that England is a country of great learning, and some of it is bound to rub off on me. All I had to do was get there."

Indeed, more explicitly, promises were given by the British government to recruits. George Powe recalls being made aware of the opportunities available after the War to potential recruits by a white officer who came to the college he was attending in search of people to join the cadets:

"The British officer told us that we would be given skills, we would be trained if we fought for the Motherland. At the end of the War, if we survived, they would see us right. In other words, they would give us land, they would extend training for those people who were at colleges and so on."

His recollection of the ethos at the time was:

"....... that the vast majority in the Westindies only wanted to get over to England; out of their own circumstances."

Hence, the recruitment campaign by the British Armed Forces tapped into a strong allegiance felt towards Britain and offered a means by which individuals could get to what they perceived as their 'Motherland'. Using propaganda concerning Nazi intentions towards black people, in conjunction with the promise of a chance to escape the economic plight that was present at the time, a rich harvest of individuals was reaped from Guyana, Jamaica, Barbados, Trinidad, and the rest of the Islands in the vicinity by way of recruitment.

RECRUITMENT

"My memory is of a huge placard somewhere in the city in which I worked. It was very glowing: 'Do you want to help the War cause?' it read, 'England needs you', with a finger pointing at you, so when you stood and looked at this thing, it became personalised. England, that great country, needs me. Of course, it had a terrific psychological effect. It didn't say that you had to have so many Junior or Senior Cambridge certificates. They only wanted you - not your qualifications. It didn't even say that you had to be fit - just, 'Do you want to serve England, your Mother Country?' And it continued: 'At this moment England is in dire trouble and so England needs you'."

The above advertisement was the recollection of one eager volunteer and was typical of the propaganda that had a powerful, galvanising impact on individuals. With the social, cultural and economic situation that existed in the Caribbean at the time, individuals were drawn in considerable numbers. The volunteer goes on to recollect that:

> "The response was terrific - overwhelming. In fact, recruitment was over-subscribed. Hundreds were turned away ..... All the ingredients for easy recruitment were present - the adverts in the press, the posters spread around the city, the excitement everywhere. Lots of boys were out of work at the time - only hanging around the streets with nothing to do. Then all of a sudden they hear that they are needed in England. That dominated their minds - not the War."

Such was the response, he adds, that when he made a late application:

> "I went grudgingly in the hope that a few might fail either the simple qualifying test or the medical test."

Ulric Cross recalls that the type of people the British government attempted to enlist in their recruitment drives was distinctly different between the start of the War and after 1944:

> "Before 1944 people did become officers or sergeants because they were aircrew, but after that, quite literally, the majority were not aircrew."

George Powe's memory of the type of individuals they sought to fill aircrew positions were the educated elite and that few of the uneducated were enlisted in that capacity.

> "They were people with degrees, that type of qualification, people who had completed their higher examinations ...... there were not many of them, perhaps about a couple of hundred."

Ulric Cross, himself an aircrew officer, verifies the perception held by George Powe:

> "One of the reasons, I suppose, there were few air-crew was that they were selected on the basis of their educational qualifications to start with. I believe, as far as I can remember, you had to have the equivalent of 5 O-levels before you could become an air-crew member. So that immediately cut out a lot of people particularly in those days in the Westindies. In Trinidad, for example, there were only two large secondary schools. Since only a very small proportion of the population had secondary education ...... only a very small percentage of people came over as aircrew."

When the recruitment was widened for groundcrew, in which the volunteers did not require specific qualifications, many more individuals were accepted. These individuals were not able to enter the RAF as aircrew men, as Ulric Cross states:

> "..... certainly I know when I joined the RAF, if you didn't have what was called Senior Cambridge Certificate, you couldn't get into the aircrew and it was as simple as that."

However, Ulric Cross felt at the time these individuals had a misconception of what their role was going to be in the RAF:

> "For most of the people, particularly those who came first as ground-crew, they didn't actually feel as though they were coming as ground-crew. They saw themselves as coming on the same basis as everybody else. They would have joined the RAF, gone through certain basic training and then they would have come over to Britain more or less to see what they were going to be."

These misconceptions by the newly enlisted may have been a result of the RAF not informing the recruits as to what their precise role was going to be in the War. George Powe, when asked to recollect what he had perceived to be his role before enlisting, confirms the ambiguity that may have existed when he states:

> "No, the only conception that I had about the War was that I would be a good fighter and nothing else."

The Jamaican government was concerned about the role its citizens were likely to be called upon to play in the War effort. Gerald Beard surmised that a political agreement had been reached between the Jamaican and the British governments limiting the role that Jamaicans would be called upon to play:

> ".... there was some scepticism by the Jamaican government. Mr Manley, at the time when we came to England, I think, was the one who was outspoken that we should not be sent to the Front. He thought it was more reasonable that the Englishmen went to the Front and we came behind, so I suppose Jamaica and the British government came to that agreement."

Individuals were not solely recruited for service in the Armed Forces. In 1941 representatives from England went to Jamaica to recruit people to work in the factories in Britain. Dudley Miller was one of many individuals who volunteered his services, with the assurance that he would not be called upon to use guns but would merely be working in the factories. Also, recruits did not only come from the Caribbean. Godfrey Petgrave, who had a Jamaican father and an Antiguan mother, enlisted in Lagos, Nigeria, August 1943. With his father at the time working in Nigeria, he recalls his entrance into the RAF:

"I saw an advert in a newspaper in Lagos, applied, took the test and passed. Out of five hundred volunteers, I was one of eight that passed and travelled to England immediately."

The advertisements for recruits to enlist in the British Forces directed individuals to a variety of places where contact could be made with the various Forces. Pasteur Irons responded to a newspaper advertisement calling for volunteers for the RAF. Stanley Hodges recalls attending the local police station and claims that he:

".... had no idea of what being an airman would be like. The excitement of going to England and seeing London and the other big cities overshadowed everything else."

One ex-serviceman stressed the voluntary nature of the recruitment in the Second World War compared to the First:

"...no one was coerced. Everyone was a volunteer, unlike the 1914-1918 War."

He goes on to recall how his father, who entered the Armed Service in the First World War, had told him of how people were informed to attend a large parade ground. These advertisements virtually mimicked a "carnival" atmosphere, contrived in order to induce people to enlist:

"They said that anyone interested should come down to The Green, which is a big parade ground, on such and such a day. They knew we liked bands and things beating, and they had a big military band which started beating marches. They said we were going to march and they marched all round the town ...... they started playing calypsos and that and we forgot all about the War.... started dancing and nobody realised that we were marching into the big police compound and, when the last man entered, the gate was closed. The Governor came out and said: 'Well, we are terribly pleased to see we have got all these people to join,' and nobody said, no. When you looked back on it, we were there whether we wanted to be or not, and then you went up and they took your name and address and all relevant details."

He continues to state that his father claimed that, although those who had been marched into the police compound knew they were being conned, nevertheless they would have been disappointed if told they could not join.

> "...you wanted to be there because if they said to you, 'Well no, you can't go,' people would have started crying because they wanted to go. But the psychology was there ..... the ruling classes at the time knew the psychology of the people they had to deal with."

Ulric Cross recalls that the contact point for individuals wanting to enter the RAF air-crew in Trinidad was via a professor at the college he was attending. This fact further re-inforces the notion that a different clientele was pursued by the RAF to fill these positions. He remembers that after making enquiries of a Professor Shephard, the professor arranged the initial contact with the appropriate authorities and eventually a flight lieutenant from the Royal Air Force was sent out to Trinidad.

Once contact was made with the RAF in England the volunteers were subjected to a number of assessments. George Powe recalls the actual process by which he was personally introduced into the RAF:

> "When I was told that they were looking for bright, intelligent youngsters to fight for the Motherland, I filled in the form. I was invited to see an officer. The officer questioned me about why I wanted to join. I told him the story that I wanted to fight. He said, 'Alright,' within a few days they would write to me and invite me for a medical examination. I went for the medical examination and I passed it, and then I was subjected to intelligence tests and I came through those tests and I was told I would be alright. The next thing I knew I was called up again about three or four days afterwards and asked to take the oath."

Gerald Beard, another ground-crewman, remembers that the intelligence test consisted of mathematics and "dictation" which was used to test the applicant's English ability. Ulric Cross, an aircrew officer, recalls that with a flight lieutenant being sent over to Trinidad, if you passed the medical and mental examination for entrance to the RAF as aircrew, then once in Britain, you could not be rejected. In many respects the sending of the flight lieutenant by the RAF ensured the right people only came over to Britain at that time as aircrew. With the groundcrew the test was not so mentally exhaustive and only needed a routinely performed exercise, as one recruit, commenting on his early days, explains:

> "Everyone was given a test and those who did not come up to educational requirements were rejected. But I must say that it wasn't very difficult and if you failed to pass it you must have been very dim. So the educational requirements were not at all strict."

However, the physical test was seen as quite a different proposition by this recruit. He recalled this assessment as originally being demanding but, as the time of departure approached, things gradually relaxed. The "dreaded" medical test he was to pass hinged on a stroke of luck and a bit of indifference and inattentiveness by the medical staff.

> "I knew I was physically fit but I was apprehensive owing to my short-sightedness. By this time I was extremely keen to join as most of my friends were joining up. I passed my medical - thanks, not to the sudden disappearance of my short-sightedness, but to the Colonial system that existed at the time. During my eye test, the white doctor sat at a table and recorded what his black assistant told him, which was not wholly the truth, but which was beneficial to me. The black assistant happened to be my next door neighbour. Had the situation been different I might never have passed. However, the perversion of the truth by the assistant meant that I was now safely on my way to England via the RAF - a situation which never in my wildest dreams could I have imagined."

Once enrolled in the services the reaction from friends and family was to question the wisdom of such action. He remembers his euphoria changing in the presence of his father and an encounter with a friend:

> "I remember quite vividly one chap, who didn't join the RAF, saying to me: 'What do you want to go and fight a war for? What will you get out of it? You have got your own country. Let the white man fight his own war.' He then proceeded to point out several jobs of which white people were the figure-heads and blacks only their lackeys. In a funny sort of way, though, I recognised some truth in what he said, I always regarded such talk as humbug, and the utterer a little short of being a crank."

George Powe had no doubts about joining the RAF while in Jamaica:

" No, my mind was open. The doubt came about when I came to England, but while I was in Jamaica I didn't have any doubt. I didn't see it in any way that I shouldn't fight. I felt that I had joined the Forces and I would try and do the best I could, become a good serviceman and fight to the best my ability. I didn't see it at the time that I was fighting for Britain. I saw it in terms of a vocation because it was something that I decided to do and I wanted to be outstanding."

Dudley Thompson says that many of his friends at the time joined up together. One of them, Adolph Thompson, who was then teaching in England, had informed him that the RAF did not enrol black colonials. Dudley Thompson goes on to express what he considered lay behind this comment and why he persisted in enlisting:

"I think he tried and was refused, but I didn't believe this and decided I was going through with it. I suppose not only natural attractiveness, but also I had my own gut feeling that the spirit of the RAF would prevail. I never at any time entertained the notion that I would not be accepted."

In a different vein, Robert Murray justified his enrolment into the RAF with the thoughts of how Nazi domination would have influenced his life.

"I did not think that playing my part in the War would gain me nothing. True, Britain was in control of Guyana and the entire Westindies at the time and certain aspects of their stewardship was far from fair. But nothing that Hitler or Mussolini did at that time suggested to me that life under them would have been any easier. Indeed, Hitler's treatment of the African-American athlete, Jesse Owens, after the 1936 Olympics in Berlin did not at all imbue me with confidence. Heaven knows what would have happened to us had they won the War. Although I did not harp on it, the thought lay secreted in the dark crevices of my mind, and this, coupled with patriotism, was where I stood."

The prospect of being subjugated by the Nazis also hovered in Dudley Thompson's mind and played a not insignificant part in influencing his decision to enlist:

"I remember picking up a copy of *The Gleaner* newspaper. I came across a part where Hitler described black people as 'having no use.' I really got annoyed at this man and his Master Race Theory. I decided I was going to move things round personally. That was my decision and that was why I enlisted. My attitude towards the War was that Britain was in trouble. We had a strong Commonwealth and if everybody in the Commonwealth pulled together we would settle the question. I, at no time, had any doubt that we would win the War. I felt this because I believed it was a just war, but we would need every man and woman whom we could muster."

As well as this factor of being subjugated by the Nazis, Dudley Thompson, in common with many other Westindian service personnel, had the conception of Britain being his Motherland, and that being the case, he considered it his bounden duty to do everything in his power to help:

"I made up my mind I wanted to enlist feeling at that time that we all had a duty towards the Mother Country; so we wanted to do our bit."

From this serviceman's point of view the RAF offered him a greater chance to contribute to the War effort. He maintains being impressed, not only with its natural attraction, but the spirit of this service.

"...... I thought that, especially in the RAF, if one became a member of it, one would be able to give a bit of one's own personal contribution to the War, more so than being in the local Forces in the Westindies. I wanted to prove for myself that, being in England, I had something to give and so I joined".

Therefore, once signed and committed to service in the Air Force, few individuals had any regrets or doubts. The recruits were contacted in various ways. Gerald Beard recalls after enlisting that he received instructions to go home and wait until a telegram arrived, which it duly did. He read it enthusiastically and then made urgent preparations:

"I packed all the necessary things that I thought I required and reported to the training camp in Jamaica."

All the recruits attended training camps in their respective countries. Gerald Beard reported to a military barracks called "Mona". Gerry

Smith, a Jamaican who enlisted in 1943, also trained at Uppark, Mona Camp. He responded to an advertisement in *The Gleaner* newspaper and still remembers the requirements:

> "You had to be vetted by a minister of Religion or a JP as to your character, and after passing the test we had twelve hours' notice before departure."

The majority of those who enlisted from Jamaica attended camp "Palisados", which was an airbase and is now called Norman Manley Airport. Since individuals were recruited from various parts of Trinidad and Tobago, Barbados, Jamaica, Guyana, and a sprinkling from the smaller Islands, St Kitts, St Lucia, Grenada, Monserrat, St Vincent etc., there existed a very strong possibility of not meeting a soul that one knew. The difficult business of making friends, for some, often proved far more disconcerting than one could imagine, for many of the recruits were hardly more than boys and some had never even left their own local areas before. However, many did come from the same localities and others teamed up with friends they had previously known from other districts. Some recruits had to make considerable journeys to reach the military barracks. Stanley Hodges recalls how he felt reassured on his journey to the camp by the presence of those he knew:

> "During my train journey to Kingston I felt delighted, and somewhat relieved, to meet other recruits on board who had volunteered the same as I had and whose destination was the same as mine."

Once they reached the camps preliminary military training became their main preoccupation as they waited for their departure to Britain. The training in many ways bore great resemblance to the sort of activities they were to undergo in Britain, with the exception of rifle and machine-gun shooting, and was performed alongside the local Army Brigade who, as recollections go, looked "a tough, seasoned lot". One remembers:

> "... the training being very hard with marches, drills, running up hill and down dale, round the parade ground and into the streets for miles and miles on end in the hot, boiling sun!"

As hitherto mentioned, the recruits hailed mainly from four different countries in the Caribbean area and the treatment meted out to some did not necessarily form the experience of others. For example, even before departure for the United Kingdom, some recruits had to eat English food in preparation for service in Europe as they were told. Others, on the other hand, indulged in their own cuisine until embarkation. The new recruits were not only ignorant regarding military life but many, because of their Caribbean background, were also not completely knowledgeable about English culture, in particular about the food that they would be eating. George Powe - possibly one of those made to sample English cuisine while still in the Caribbean - remembers the recruits alongside him being upset by the fact that they were given unfamiliar English food: potatoes, carrots, cabbage etc., to eat. Not that the Westindians had never heard of 'Greens and Vegetables'. On the contrary, such foods occasionally formed part of their diet - but done to their liking, with a far less preponderance of water. He continues to state that his mates often felt victimized because they did not understand Service discipline, instancing one personal experience to illustrate his point:

> "I found myself in a queue waiting for my uniform and talking to a friend when a sergeant approached and told me to shut up or else.... The next thing I knew, he ordered me to get out of the queue at the double. I didn't know what doubling meant so I stood there. Then, in a more furious outburst, he commanded me to double! Anyway, he must have realised that I didn't have the foggiest idea what he was saying so he calmed down and showed me what doubling meant - to run up and down until he told me stop ......He then intimated that the next time such a thing occurred I would be put on a charge. That was my first experience and I remember, at that precise moment, regretting joining the service".

The recruits were still in training in the Westindies while everyone remained expectant about the imminent departure which could not be delayed much longer. However, the Military Authorities, in an effort to keep the movement of service personnel secret, sought to suppress any possible news of departure. Nevertheless during the run-up to sailing to UK, there were periods in which the training took the recruits beyond the camp's periphery into the full glare of the civilian population. Even after all these years the memory is still alive with the occasion when the public had incorrectly anticipated the servicemen's departure. This event occurred the day before the sailing, although the time still defied prediction. One ex-serviceman reflects:

> "We went on a long parade round the city ending up at one of the local cinemas. I will never forget the scenes on the streets till the day I die. It seemed as if the entire population of the capital had turned out to say their goodbyes. Fathers, mothers, relatives and friends - particularly girlfriends - were in tears. Many felt they would not see their loved ones again as the War would claim them. At the cinema we saw the film, Holiday Inn, starring Bing Crosby. The recruits all enjoyed it and came out once again to face the multitudinous crowd who followed us all the way back to the barracks. We should have guessed that our departure was nigh."

Pasteur Irons enlisted in Jamaica in 1943 and was among the first Westindian ground-crew airmen destined to serve in the United Kingdom. He remembers the occasion well. The intelligence test was exacting and his medical examination, in the presence of three doctors, had been most rigid. Unemployment in the Westindies at that time had reached astronomical proportions and this forced hundreds to answer the call to enlist, but it was a case of many being called and few chosen. The tests - particularly the intelligence test caused a vast number to fall by the wayside:

> "Unfortunately, hundreds did not succeed, failing at least one of the tests. Standards, for my batch, had to be high because they had many to choose from, each one of the successful applicants being outstanding. We were regarded as the 'Cream'. I heard that the standard subsequently dropped for other groups that followed."

Although the actual time for embarkation and sailing to the UK remained a closely guarded secret, some of the enlisted men were allowed "embarkation" leave during which they were allowed home to visit relatives and friends.

Even though the Military Authorities had recruited nearly as many volunteers as required, there were sometimes circumstances beyond their control that kept eroding acquired numbers. An example of such an eventuality occurred when a successful applicant became ill to such an extent as to cast doubts on his ability to travel. A recruit who suffered such an experience relates:

> "After enlisting, I suddenly developed an abscess under my right arm. This was very painful and caused the military authorities a great deal of concern because departure was imminent. I was in a state of panic fearing that I would easily be dropped at the very last minute in favour of one of the many who had been turned away as surplus to requirements; but no, to my great delight they had my abscess lanced and within a day or two I was as right as rain."

Another reason - perhaps the main reason - was that sailing of troop-carrying vessels had to be synchronized with the movement of other convoy ones - corvettes, frigates, submarines and destroyers gathering in the Atlantic and collecting ships from the various Islands in the Caribbean. So it was believed that those in command of the Forces were reluctant to contact and assess new recruits forcing the conclusion that:

> ".... whether you were ill or not, at this stage you had to go."

Although the recruits knew that they were destined for Britain and were kept in the dark as to the precise time when they were to depart, they were nevertheless shocked when the time came - shocked at the abrupt manner and speed of the operation. On reflection, Gerald Beard states:

> ".... suddenly we were ordered to pack our kit bags because the boat was in harbour awaiting us. We had no alternative but to comply with that order."

For another recruit, it was a time of scares and false alarms about the departure whereby they went to bed at "lights out" in full battle order, were aroused in the early hours of the morning, ushered on the parade ground for a roll call and then ordered back to bed again, the whole exercise always being described as a false alarm. Such exercises invariably found disfavour as sleep did not always revisit easily - particularly in the tropics and in full uniform of course. The whole idea served to keep the recruits on full alert and in a high state of preparedness. On the other hand, the frequency of such exercises provoked a certain amount of incredulity, so that when the real departure time arrived after so many rehearsals naturally the recruits were "taken off guard". The mind is effervescent with details of the occasion as one who experienced it reminds how they attempted to leave the camp unnoticed and embark on the journey to Britain:

> "That night, lights-out was at 9.30 p.m. Then, at about 3 o'clock in the morning, the orders, loud and clear, came to rise and shine. We were already dressed apart from our boots, so we were all lined up outside at the ready. All our rucksacks and heavy gear were in trucks. Then the instructions came in whispers so as to avoid peremptory commands at so early an hour. 'We're going on a route march, boys. Move along in broken footsteps. Do not march, and talk quietly.' What extraordinary instructions! Of course, no way could military detachments proceed through the streets at that hour in the morning without attracting attention. People opened their windows and even doors to witness this curious spectacle straddling along. Everyone wanted to come out to say their goodbyes and to wish us good luck - the very thing the military authorities sought to prevent. Some even followed us on the way to the docks. We went aboard quickly and in a short time were on our way."

Westindian women, too, played their part in the last War, although their numbers were not comparable to those of the Westindian men enlisted; perhaps their numbers exceeded no more than a hundred in all the services. However, they performed sterling work, being represented in most skills in the three main women's services - The Women's Royal Army Corps (WRACS), The Women Auxiliary Air Force (WAAFS) and the Women Royal Naval Services (WRNS) - not to mention the nursing and other services. In fact, their work and commitment to the Second World War bore such importance that no publication purporting to deal with the subject of Westindian involvement in the conflict would be complete without reference being made to their contribution. The women - mere girls at the time being in their late teens or early twenties, hailed mostly from elite backgrounds and were highly educated. Girls like Norma Best (nee Leacock) Nadia Kattouse and Carol Campbell from Belize (then British Honduras); Hyacinth Thame, Myrtle Heron, Esther Armagon (nee McMorris) and Hazel Armagon (nee Taylor) from Jamaica; and

Margot Senson and Gwen Eytle from Guyana. All the girls with the exception of Carol Campbell joined up around June 1944. The Guyanese and Belizians journeyed to the Army Headquarters at Pallisadoes Jamaica for their initial training. Most enlisted in the Auxiliary Territorial Service (ATS). Norma Best recalls her military training as "being very tough - especially, the marching."

Not all the girls enjoyed the luxury of free transport to Jamaica to be trained. A few like Carol Campbell, had to make their own arrangements for travelling. She had been unfortunate to miss selection with the batch of girls recruited in Belize. Nevertheless, resolved not be defeated and determined not to wait for any subsequent recruitment drive to gain entry, she travelled to America under her own steam, contacted the British Embassy there and they, gratified by her courage and tenacity, felt moved to have her transported to the United Kingdom where she hoped to enlist in one of the many women's services available.

> Meanwhile, all the other girls doing their initial training in Jamaica were looking forward to journeying to the UK to excitement, adventure and 'joie de vivre!'

JOURNEY TO THE UNITED KINGDOM

The passage to Britain took different routes according to whether the recruits formed part of the aircrew or members of the groundcrew. There was a distinct difference between the two. Most members of the aircrew received their training in Canada and many passed out as commissioned officers. A small number of aircrew members obtained their training in England. However, whether trained in Canada or England, no aircrew member passed out with a rank lower than sergeant.

Another difference was that most aircrew personnel enlisted in the early 1940s while groundcrew staff mainly joined from 1943. On the other hand, the transportation of the groundcrew recruits tended to follow the same pattern. Those from Guyana, Barbados and the smaller islands assembled in Trinidad, picked up the Trinidadians and then on to Jamaica where the Jamaicans boarded before heading for the United Kingdom via America except for the last batch that proceeded by way of Bermuda after leaving Jamaica. The groundcrew into which the vast majority of Westindians enlisted, performed some initial training in the Caribbean and this was augmented by further military training in the UK. Of the four batches of Westindian recruits to reach the United Kingdom, three arrived on various dates during 1944 and one arrived early in 1945; but the journey across difficult and often hazardous seas, still hovers in the memory to this day! Pasteur Irons, who was travelling with the very first batch of Jamaicans in the SS Cuba, remembers the sea being very rough and boisterous. They experienced the worst sea conditions imaginable:

> "We were convoyed by two American destroyers until arriving in the USA. We spent 12 days there at Camp Patrick Henery in Newport News, Virginia. Then one morning, off the coast of Newfoundland, we woke to one of the most breathtaking sights we'd ever witnessed - an array of protection vessels of every description stretching as far as the eye could see. To the eye of youngsters, this was a most exciting and

impressive sight 'Troopships, cargo boats and tankers in the middle of the formation with battleships, cruisers, destroyers, frigates, corvettes on the outside - at times far in the distance - a real marvel and a sight to bolster the spirits of the security-conscious! The message to all enemy vessels seemed to proclaim - 'Danger, Beware!'. It was a marvel! Later on, nearer our destination, the sea became tempestuous and we all felt ill at times."

The recruits that walked in broken footsteps and boarded their ship quickly in the previous chapter were all Guyanese who formed part of the very last batch to be leaving for the United Kingdom, this being late in December 1944, and the War finished in 1945. Their immediate destination - although, because of War secrecy, they remained ignorant of it at the time - was Trinidad where they were to join Barbadians, those from the smaller islands and the Trinidadians. Two ex-servicemen, Alwyn Pindar and Frank Holders still have memories of the sailing from Guyana. Pindar says:

"As all the familiar landmarks became smaller and smaller many of the boys wept and it was then one realised that one was going to war. However, as soon as the last of the landmarks had faded away, Guyana was forgotten - albeit for the time being."

Experience aboard a troopship differed considerably depending on who was in command - in other words whether the servicemen were aboard a British or an American ship. Life on the American ship seemed brimful with entertainment as Frank Holder, himself aspiring to follow the entertainment business after the War, would not forget:

"On the American ship, they were all out for enjoyment. In those days the Jive and Boogie Woogie were in fashion and they got us jiving. 'Come on, guys', they would encourage.... let's go, man, let's go! And they soon got us jiving, bebopping and hopping around like mad."

He observed that the Americans did not bother too much about the War. 'Enjoy yourself now' seemed to be their motive - even though there could have been German U-boats or destroyers around. The fact that so many servicemen were on board did not seem to matter. They seemed totally preoccupied with enjoyment. Neither, it was observed, did they seem to take any notice of colour, treating the recruits in a different manner to their own blacks. "Fortunately," continued Holder, "we suffered no surprise attacks during our crossing. "The friendliness of the Americans left the Caribbean servicemen perplexed and befuddled after hearing stories about the racist attitudes of the Americans. Another occasion on which the Americans contradicted this widely held view was at Camp Patrick Henery in the south of America as Pasteur Irons concurs:

> "While their negroes were hanging around outside the dancehall, our boys were given a good time, invited in and told to enjoy themselves which seemed amazing considering the way they treated their own blacks. It seemed they regarded us Westindians as guests being subjects of His Majesty King George VI."

Some servicemen sometimes experienced very long waits before continuing their journey as those in the last batch experienced in Trinidad. The stay there lasted for about three months and nobody was told any reasons for the delay - although most recruits suspected it had to do with convoys - the movement of troops not being permitted without protection vessels being in escort. George Haynes, one of the Barbadians at St James's Camp, Port of Spain, at the time states:

> "We all surmised that the wait had something to do with convoys - those corvettes, destroyers, frigates and other protection vessels. Troops could not be moved without these being in attendance and sometimes it took time for them to get into position."

These periods of waiting for convoys were never wasted, being spent mostly on training, and one devoted the rest of the time to other healthy pursuits such as athletics. Indeed, as many who were there would agree, it was the time in their lives when they were at their fittest. Delving back in the dark recesses of the memory, one thinks of E. McDonald-Bailey, himself a Trinidadian and one of the outstanding athletes of the day and who represented England in the 1948 Olympics, running some of the boys off their feet having given them substantial starts in the 'sprint races'. Very few realised then that those 'fun races' heralded the precursors of an exciting athletic career for McDonald-Bailey (Mac, as he was then called).

But one also recalls this waiting period being very boring because the recruits were deterred from socializing, for their own well being, with the civilian population. With hundreds of other troops around, the risk of contracting diseases was very great, hence the need for complete abstinence, as the reminiscences of an ex-serviceman reveal:

> "So our wait was long and sometimes boring - boring because most of our off-duty periods were spent in camp. We were warned not to go out and pick up any disease as we would be sent home. This warning frightened everybody. No one wanted to get this far and then return home in disgrace. So everyone had to exercise the strictest control over himself - keeping his grisle firmly imprisoned in his trousers."

The ground crew recruits, irrespective of which batch they were drafted into, could hardly ever forget the English NCOs who put them through their initial training in the Caribbean and in whose charge the boys spent a great part of their time whether on or off the parade ground. These NCOs gave the boys several pep-talks about what life in England would be like. Most of them were tough and well-seasoned, having been seconded to the RAF from the RAF Regiment. Many of the recruits knew the NCOs by name - being aware of their foibles, their strengths and their dispositions. The recruits biding their time in Trinidad and Tobago saw quite a lot of these NCOs. Vernon Hunte, a Trinidadian who joined at the last minute because of late discards, remembers a Corporal Keyworth and a Corporal Sergeant while the memories of others are still alive with the names of Flight Sergeant Downey, Sergeant Foster (nicknamed 'Poots' because of an impediment in his speech causing him to pronounce the letter B as P), Corporal Charlton and Corporal Wilkinson, (who was very young at the time). Most of the pep-talks were often quite informative as well as being humorous. But, on the eve of their departure for the UK, something was said by one of the NCO's which, not only incurred the wrath of the recruits but gave them forewarning of the attitudes and confrontations awaiting them in Britain.

The NCO started off by telling the lads that when they arrived in the UK they shouldn't expect the things they were used to...Rice and

Peas, Bajee Bush, Beef Curry and all that sort of stuff. His utterances sounded less like information and more like 'laying down the law'. This forecast hit the recruits badly enough but they found his next prediction absolutely devastating:

> " 'Don't think you're going there to paint the town red .... No woman there would consort with you!' "

It was difficult for the recruits to grasp what had presaged this comment as they sought to find reason for such prognostication.

> None of the boys could imagine just what had prompted such an outburst for, until this point, relations between NCOs and men could only have been described as cordial.

The NCO's prognostications and the manner of deliverance elicited strong resentment - albeit silently - being, for the recruits, the first encounter with the British in the field of what they conceived to be the issue of 'colour'. More particularly, they sensed the advent of racial overtones in the reference to women whom all construed to be 'non-black women'.

Despite long, historical links, most Westindians had never before encountered Englishmen at grass roots level and, quite apart from displays of superiority and arrogance at times, the boys had no previous social experience to serve as a guide. For the vast majority this was the first real intercourse with the 'English', who, because of the hierarchical colonial structure that existed, very rarely permitted inter-racial contact. Even though the native Westindian might have been suitably skilled or qualified, he had to be subjugated to the Englishman and this fact could not be forgotten. It could well have provided the catalyst that fuelled the NCO's damaging pronouncements.

Neither was this latest misunderstanding about 'colour' the first to involve this particular senior NCO. One recalls the occasion in Guyana when he received a severe reprimand for failing to salute a black officer in the local army there. Many more confrontations on this issue were to manifest themselves to many of the Westindian servicemen - especially with white Americans. The NCO's comments predictably caused consternation amongst the recruits, leaving them in a state of disbelief and with a very adverse impression. However, being subordinates, they could do nothing apart from feel aggrieved: but they did display signs of 'dumb insolence' by the 'knitting of eyebrows and the sucking of teeth', characteristics then unknown to the British NCOs. An ex-serviceman, looking back on the incident, describes the prevailing moods thus:

> "It was as though life at that moment had come to a standstill. A deathly silence descended amongst the boys for a few minutes. Each looked at the other askance. For a man to make such a statement, even if it were true, having previously said, 'We were going home to the Mother Country just didn't gel with us and we tucked it away at the backs of our minds for future reference!"

Food was a topic which always predominated and one which would continuously be cropping up. Ordinarily, the subject would carry no significance at all if service were to be performed in the Caribbean; but in a country whose cuisine contrasted sharply with that which the recruits were accustommed to, there was almost bound to be constant comparison and often, disapprobation. Gerald Beard, a Jamaican, who arrived in the U.K. in 1944 and who found it difficult to cope with the food initially, states:

> "I, myself, took it very badly because the food just wasn't good enough; it made no difference whether one complained or not as you'd get the same thing...!"

But the food did not always meet with disapproval. Those recruits who sailed on the American troopship from Guyana to Trinidad would never forget the excellent food they enjoyed on board.

Although a war raged on, only certain imported foods or foodstuffs were in short supply in their country, but local forms of nourishment existed in abundance. No one, therefore, suffered any starvation. On the American ship, however, they saw food of quality and in quantity, the like of which they had never witnessed before. Two of the lads on board, Frank Holder and Alwyn Pindar, reminisce. Frank Holder opines:

"What impressed me the most was the presentation. Each man was served on a tray consisting of a segment for each item of the meal. At breakfast, for example, each little compartment held its own eggs (two), bacon, sausages, tomatoes, bread, grapefruit or other fruit plus juice in addition to cereal and this was not all. You could have had as many helpings as you wanted. One simply indulged oneself."

Alwyn Pindar reflects:

"Well, we just never saw that kind of breakfast back home. Eggs, bacon and sausage were scarce at the time but the Yanks had plenty."

And yet another ex-serviceman, Robert Murray, still enthuses over the Five Star Hotel-like 'nosh' on that boat:

"I was a big eater and thoroughly enjoyed myself, downing not only my own share, but several others' as well - especially when they became sea-sick, as they often were."

George Powe, recruited earlier in the War and who would have travelled on a different ship, had a somewhat dissimilar experience:

"We ate up all the food because there wasn't a lot of it. After about ten days we ran out of food and they had to change course for Ireland to replenish the food stocks."

At last the long laborious wait at the camp in Port of Spain, Trinidad, came to an abrupt end. No one had any time to think. Suddenly, 200 Guyanese, 200 Trinidadians and Tobagons plus a miscellany of Barbadians, Kiticians, St Lucians, Dominicans, Grenadians, Antiguans etc., found themselves afloat and bound for Jamaica. Everyone felt happy to be on the move again - even though the seas held dangers with German U-boats about but thoughts of any mishaps never entered the recruits' heads. Their youthful exuberance would not allow them to think of danger - only of excitement, adventure and arrival in the UK! The final batch of Westindian airmen were now pounding the seas in a British ship, a massive vessel, the HMS Carthage, equipped to carry thousands of men and with powerful guns fore and after. In contrast to the experience aboard the American troopship, where enjoyment dominated, observations on the ethos on the British ship brought into sharp focus the difference in attitudes. Unlike the American ship, the discipline was strict, businesslike and, above all, imbued one with a sense of security.

The troopship, HMS Carthage was steadily making its way towards Jamaica with the eager recruits. For the following months this colossal vessel was to become their abode - akin to the homes they had left behind. In the words of one ex-airman:

> "We were told that that was our living quarters until we reached our destination."

Meanwhile those in charge were exercising their minds on what to do on arrival at Jamaica, concluding that it would be folly to permit hundreds of fit, young men deprived of female companionship for months to land there. Not that such an action would have been a departure from precedence. Bob Roach, who was born in Barbados but brought up in Trinidad and who enlisted in April 1944, remembers his batch being allowed ashore in Jamaica. They did a route march, but were not given shore leave because the authorities felt they couldn't take the risk fearing that the recruits might not observe the strict time schedule for their return to the ship.

As the magnificent views of the beautiful island of Jamaica came into sight from the ship which was now keeping a fair distance from the shore, the boys could see women and girls picking bananas, plantains and tropical fruits, carrying them in baskets on their heads, their hips swaying as they moved along, sending the boys' temperatures soaring several degrees higher. They fancied the fruits as well as the girls while strong, persuasive efforts had to be exerted to discourage some of the enthusiasts from taking to water in pursuit of their prey! As it was, they had to be content with feasting their eyes, waving and emitting wolf-whistles.'

The shrewdness of the military authorities kept the troopship in mid-stream while the Jamaicans came aboard from smaller vessels. Some were big fellows and they out-numbered the Guyanese, Trinidadians, Barbadians and others by more than two to one. The discipline had to 'be tight'.

The assembly of such a vast number of Westindian recruits was augmented by a much larger contingent of Americans and Canadians who, according to rumour, were destined to fight the Japanese in the Far East. This piece of information came as good news to the boys from the Caribbean who had earlier been given to understand from a somewhat spurious source that the Orient was their destination.

The movement of such a large number of military personnel resulted in the gathering of an assortment of ships which descended and dispersed swiftly and were not necessarily making for Europe. Athleston Holder, a Jamaican, remembers:

> "Then one morning we woke up to be surrounded by a miscellany of ships - warships, corvettes, destroyers, troopers carrying thousands of men, mostly Americans to the Far East. Then the following morning they were all gone - vanished as fast as they had appeared."

The spectacle of a medley of ships, some armed to the teeth, bulging with men, and moving with belligerent intent, filled many with trepidation and bewilderment. Yet, such bewilderment was tinged with the reassurance, emphasizing the fact that safety remained paramount.

The paradoxical nature of these ships of war left a salient impression on all. The gracefulness and eloquence with which they glided across the ocean, juxtaposed with their purpose - to impose peace and yet prepared to unleash deadly implements of war at a moment's notice. One ex-airman correctly typifies the paradox as he reflects:

> "We looked upon the vast Armada - ships peacefully sailing, minding their own business, yet with hostile intentions!"

Whilst very few of the recruits entertained any thoughts of disaster, the threat of enemy attack never strayed very far from the minds of those in charge of the ship and this fact manifested itself in the frequent boat-drills with life-jackets at the ready. Looking back upon it now, one wonders what would have happened in the face of an attack! There did not appear to be enough life-boats for about 1,500 men and crew; what would have happened if the order had come to abandon ship? The thought of jumping into freezing, cold water fully uniformed with heavy boots on seemed far too ghastly to contemplate. One felt confident and cosy surrounded by a multiplicity of protective vessels, but there were many times when no such protection could be seen - although one was assured that help was never too far away. James Mckenzie, a Jamaican, who travelled in 1944, speaks in retrospect:

> "The voyage was good with good food and entertainment but there were moments which caused fear and anxiety as there were many German submarines all around us. This caused some panic - but only for a little while. Then all was calm again."

Stan Hodges remembers hearing:

> "Gunfire in the distance. Fortunately our convoy escort succeeded in fighting off the German U-boat without any casualties being reported. It was then I realised I was really at war!"

Frank Holder recollects seeing tracer-bullets being fired, although he could not remember if it was an exercise or an actual attack! George Powe attempts to characterize some of the boys who used to try to impress everyone that they were brave - those boys who would stick their chests out and boast about what they would do if they saw the enemy:

> "But what was remarkable was, when there were rumours of U-boats in the area, a lot of chaps who while on camp pretended to be brave and bullies, started crying and calling for their mothers. Few of us were over twenty years of age and a lot of the youngsters were still attached to their parents; this and the fact that they had never left home before, distressed them somewhat, causing them to make a fuss. Apart from the menace of German U-boats and submarines in conjunction with periodic raging, mountainous seas, other incidents sometimes occured to jangle the nerves. Very little happened during the dark nights or early mornings - only the heavy drumming of the ship's engines together with its perpetual rolling and tossing - to cause the recruits any concern. Nevertheless, one morning about three o'clock, while all slumbered away, a sudden screaming accosted the air, followed by a commotion with everyone rushing around in a state of drunken stupor, making for the upper decks with life-jackets on prepared to carry out the rehearsed routine for times of emergency. As no explosion had been heard there

was a state of confusion as to what had happened. Then, to great disbelief and annoyance, it transpired that one Guyanese was having a nightmare in which a snake had wrapped itself around his neck causing him to shout out in his sleep: 'Cobra, cobra,' tearing at his throat. The rest of the recruits gave a lengthy moan and set about the culprit with a verbal assault, being, at the same time, thankful that nothing more hostile had occurred - no bombs, no torpedoes, only a dream. They all turned and trooped back down below to their bunks to resume their broken slumber. Needless to say, the perpetrator took a very long time to live that down."

Shortly after that incident the ship docked in Bermuda to pick up the North Atlantic Convoy. Very shortly afterwards, the journey was continued. The unbridled power of the sea took the recruits by surprise and at times caused them a little more than concern. Most of them, being Islanders, would almost certainly have seen the sea before but not many would have experienced its venom before. It's one thing standing on shore and gazing out on the sea. It's another thing sailing on it when it is in uproarious mood. It's ferocity, at times, filled some of the servicemen with terror and awe, forcing those with sensitive stomachs to seek shelter in their bunks and, as George Powe previously observed, many were big, powerfully-built lads - the sort who commanded respect on dry land because of their size, but who soon became 'jelly' as soon as the ship's engines began to 'purr!'

Two Westindians among those approaching the coast of Britain in early 1945 were Athleston Holder (Jamaica) and George Haynes (Barbados). Both give their recollections. Holder says:

"Crossing to England was extremely rough. Waves reached extraordinary heights, tossing the huge ship around like a match-box."

And George Haynes states:

"On our way to England I can remember encountering seas, the like of which I never thought existed. We were in this enormous vessel, the HMS. Carthage, which was being pitched from 'pillar to post'. Sometimes I felt that it would break into pieces. For most of us, it was our first journey by sea and, at times, it was frightening. Somehow we got to the English Channel where some of the worst weather was experienced. Winds of unbelievable ferocity provoking waves of breathtaking heights causing the ship to rock, roll and shudder violently, listing at seemingly impossible angles!"

Meanwhile the ATS girls who had assembled at Uppark Camp, Mona, Jamaica to undergo their initial training, had completed it and were now continuing their journey to the UK via America. Norma Best distinctly recollects the crossing from Jamaica being:

"As good as one could have expected at the time - very scary, but exciting."

Esther Armagon, in the same batch, recalls how they were kitted out in New Orleans and, from there, proceeded by pullman train to New York where they spent a little time in Central Park before joining the twin of the famous Sister Liners - The Queen Mary - on the final stage of their journey. There were about 30 girls altogether in this particular batch and they travelled with a full consignment of Canadian soldiers.

These girls now nearing the shores of Britain formed part of a group of about 100 Westindian women who were permitted to join the British Forces from about 1943. Before that time there was a definite policy to keep them out of Britain. As early as 1941 applications from Caribbean women to join the British Forces - and especially the ATS - had either been suppressed or flatly refused. A war, fiercer than that of the actual conflict itself, raged between the War Office and the Colonial Office. The War Office offered every excuse to deter the women from enlisting - excuses such as the British climate, cultural differences, their own environment was better and, finally, lack of shipping space, an argument even ensued as to the paying of the women's fares to the UK. They were adamant that no black Westindian woman would serve during the War in Britain. The War Office even suggested that it was impossible to employ Westindian women on normal pay and allowances; they should receive less. The Colonial Office, on the other hand, argued strongly, largely through Harold Macmillan, then a Minister in that office, that Britain's best interest would be served by involving the colonies in the War; a Westindian Pioneer Unit would be good and would serve to bind that region more closely to the Mother Country.

In the meantime there were a few incidents which were silently simmering away and which, when fully boiled, would hasten the day when black Westindian women would be admitted into the British Forces to serve in Britain. At the RAF mission in Washington, where only whites were employed, applications were received from 16 women from the Bahamas to join the Women's Auxiliary Air Force (WAAF), and the RAF, therefore, found itself in a quandary; while not wanting to accept any black women, it was conscious the political backlash that might follow from a refusal of their applications. The Governor of the Bahamas at the time was none other than His Royal Highness, The Duke of Windsor, who was pressurizing the Colonial Office to have the women's applications processed as a matter of urgency. However, when it subsequently transpired that the Bahamian applicants happened to be of European stock and of the 'right type', the Air Ministry dropped its objections and was prepared to accept them. But this was not the end of the matter as the women wanted to be attached to the RAF mission in Washington which operated a 'colour bar'. There was deadlock. Further, when it was pointed out that acceptance of white Westindians might encourage applications from non-whites who, if refused, might cause serious repercussions, the RAF was prepared to exclude the whites in the pursuance of their racial policy, and in their pandering to Washington. After the fracture that would be caused to Westindian and UK relations was revealed to the Air Ministry, they now relented and were prepared to tolerate an arrangement in which whites worked in Washington and blacks in the Caribbean. To this arrangement, the then Governor of Barbados, Sir Henry G Bushe, was the first to object, informing the Secretary of State for the Colonies in January, 1943, that such a situation would cause resentment in the Caribbean and urged him to reconsider the matter in the interest of racial harmony. When, finally, Westindian women were allowed to work in Washington and in England, they were adjudged to be of "excellent quality," had adjusted admirably to conditions in Britain and had well and truly proved themselves in spite of the bitter battle to keep them out. Their path to service in Britain had certainly not been smooth.

ARRIVALS AND RECEPTION IN BRITAIN

As it would be deduced from this book Westindians entered the Royal Air Force either as aircrew or as groundcrew. Those joining as aircrew, did so in the early part of the war, some even paying their own fare either to the UK or to Canada where they were trained.

Billy Strachan, mentioned earlier, left Jamaica for England at the age of 18, intent on joining the RAF - his boyhood dream. Arriving at Bristol on a wet Saturday in March, 1940 with £3 in his pocket, one suitcase containing a change of clothes.

Although he knew no one, he felt convinced that the world was his oyster as he caught the first train for London. Spending the night at the only place whose name he'd encountered before - the YMCA in Tottenham Court Road which cost him one shilling:

"On Monday morning I presented myself at the Air Ministry which, I thought, must be the place where you joined up; but when I knocked at the door, I was told to go away, first by the guards then in even stronger terms, by a sergeant. I argued with them, attracting the attention of a passing officer who said, "I learnt geography at school and I think you West Africans are wonderful. Come along with me."

Something bordering on pandemonium ensued when Billy gave his birth place as Kingston, Surrey, which only the friendly officer deciphered as being in Kingston, Surrey, Jamaica, and not Kingston, Surrey, England.

The joining-up formalities were soon dispensed with, a medical examination hastily arranged and very shortly afterwards the overjoyed recruit found himself on a train enroute for Blackpool and 12 weeks of basic wireless operator training.

It will be seen that various forms of sea transport were used to get the Westindians - men and women - into Britain during the War - conventional ships, British and American, troopships, even luxury liners. Despite all the exigences of the War, no one was ever left behind because of lack of transport. Pasteur Irons, whose batch travelled to America in the SS Cuba in the spring of 1944, continued the journey to the UK in a different ship, the HMT Harrower, a New Zealand vessel in which the space was shared between the Westindian recruits and New Zealand troops. At times, even enemy vessels had to be pressed into commission. Gerald Beard recalls that the ship in which he travelled to the UK had been an old German one.

As previously mentioned, except for a few individuals who made their own way to Britain and joined various services, the vast majority of Westindians were enlisted into the RAF groundcrew from about 1943 - a period of very high unemployment in the region. The question may well be posed, therefore, as to why, given such an unlimited source of manpower, recruitment remained unexploited for such a long period after the commencement of hostilities when such a dire need existed for all the help necessary. The appropriate answer might well be found at the end of the previous chapter - the operation of the British Colour Bar!

The ports at which Westindian groundcrew recruits arrived into Britain depended to a certain extent on the particular batch to which they were drafted. Similarly, their reception on arrival varied for reasons which were not quite apparent at the time. However, although there was never a flag-waving, euphoric crowd to welcome the recruits, there always seemed to be some form of reception in waiting for them.

Mainly two ports of arrival were used - Liverpool and Greenock on the river Clyde in Scotland; and of the four major groups of groundcrew personnel, two arrived in June, 1944, one in November, 1944, and the last in March, 1945. Here are the recollections of the very first impressions of England as seen through the eyes of some of the then servicemen: Carl Brewster (Barbados), Bob Roach (Trinidad & Tobago) and Stanley Hodges (Jamaica) sailed up the Mersey (Liverpool) early in June, 1944 in the HMS Esperance Bay. Bob Roach remembers that, because of the circuitous route the ship had to take, he still felt the cold north winds in his bones - even though it was summer. All three have memories of being welcomed by an RAF band and Sir Oliver Stanley, the then Colonial Secretary.

Carl Brewster was shocked to see the difference in lifestyle between England and the Westindies where simple commodities like cigarettes, sweets, ordinary items of clothing and foodstuffs were readily available compared to England. Shortages were evident everywhere and the hardships that people were undergoing came home to him quite forcibly. Pasteur Irons, whose batch arrived before the end of June, 1944, in the HMT Harrower, also docked in Liverpool and was equally welcomed by a band and Sir Oliver Stanley. Even a very high - ranking RAF officer was there to greet them. Pasteur Irons found himself mystified by what appeared to be 'periscopes' sticking out of the roofs of houses in the distance and which he found out later to be chimneys. He had never seen any in Jamaica and wondered what they were. Another piece of wonderment to those recruits was the sight of women working on the railway stations as porters and other unskilled forms of labour - a 'phenomenon' they would never have witnessed back home. Pasteur Irons states that, on arrival, as the various forms of transport flashed by portraying advertisements of different brand names, he and his companions were vying with each other to see who could guess first in which part of England the products were manufactured. Indeed, so thorough was their knowledge gained through school, books, periodicals and magazines that they could pinpoint most products made in England just by their names. So great was the feeling about, and interest in, the 'Mother Country', that any knowledge nurtured about Her was savoured with pride.

The recruits just docked in Liverpool were now safely on their way bound for Filey near Scarborough in Yorkshire which, before the War, used to be a holiday camp. En route, they had time to gaze through the windows and drink in the English countryside for the very first time. They reflected, too, on their respective countries and the homes they had left behind - parents, relatives, friends. They probably were thinking of how they came to be travelling in a train in England heading for their first training camp. It had taken some of them a long time to get to this point from the date of their original application. Just a mere 18 months previously, if anyone had predicted they would have been in the Royal Air Force heading for a military destination in the 'Mother Country', they would have dismissed such a prediction as folly and impossible. Now each delved into recollections of the past few months. As the train huffed, puffed and chugged its way along - for those were the days of steam

- Pasteur Irons was probably thinking about his father in Jamaica who was vehemently opposed to his son joining the RAF and departing to the UK because of the treatment meted out to Jamaicans who joined up in the 1914-18 War when people were killed and maimed without anything being done for them or their relatives.

Together with American and Canadian troops, the next batch of Westindians - George Powe and Gerald Beard included - entered the UK in the Autumn of 1944, again by way of Greenock on the River Clyde. George Powe reflects:

> "It was raining and we were greeted by a lively band. There were a number of WRACS present who kept us warm with cups of tea and coffee - for we found it extremely cold. Shortly afterwards we were put on troop-trains for our training camp in Filey. We thought it funny that some people were asking for cigarettes, stockings etc. Newly arrived from the Caribbean, the idea of rationing had not yet come home to us. It was a novelty, the operation of which had to be experienced to be appreciated. We had no knowledge of it in the Caribbean, though we soon learnt the necessity for it in Britain."

Other arrivals experienced varying forms of reception. Eric Hudson, Athleston Holder, Vernon Hunte, Frank Holder, Alwyn Pindar and Robert Murray all formed part of the fourth and final batch to sail up the Clyde and dock at Greenock in March, 1945. They did not have the cheering effects of a band to greet them, though an Air Ministry Official was present. Alwyn Pindar remembers this Official:

> "He seemed very staid in demeanour and was very brief. 'Welcome to the United Kingdom,' he said. 'You boys have come a long way to help us. Thank you very much.' And that was that. But the WVS (Women's Voluntary Service) were there in full strength to greet us. Again, these were the first white people we'd seen in such a capacity, that is, serving us, rather than the other way round. They were extremely pleasant, pouring out cups of hot brew and dishing out the biscuits with gusto, chatting, singing and joking as they did so. Their ebullience became contagious to such an extent that it buoyed us up, contributing a great deal to the reduction of our homesickness and melancholy."

And Robert Murray's introduction to what he perceived to be his 'Motherland' remains indelibly engraved on his mind - that of darkness, coldness and fogginess!

"A heavy mist hung over the Clyde and it looked dismal, forbidding and unfriendly. Men in boats all around us could hardly be discerned - in fact, one sensed their presence rather that saw them, because of the thick mist. We all felt distinctly cold. I can vividly recall saying to a friend: 'This seems a very alien and frigid land'. Our first inclination was to turn around, there and then, and make for home. Having just left the Caribbean - the land of sunshine - there was no sun, no heat here, only cold, gloom and, seemingly dark desolation!"

However, though everyone thought of it, all knew that to do an about-turn then was virtually impossible. They had volunteered to help - and help they had to - whatever the adversities. Further, if even it were possible to return home immediately, how could they tell friends and relatives at home that they'd quit because of the climate? They would have been ridiculed, laughed to scorn and branded as "chicken!" They had arrived and were going to be in the British Isles for the duration of the present emergency, as they were constantly being reminded. If return had been a real choice, very few would have elected to desert and would have preferred to stay to see the thing through. After all, they had seen nothing yet.

This fourth and final batch of Westindian RAF groundcrew intakes now boarded a train destined, not for Filey in Yorkshire as was the case with previous groups, but for Melksham in Wiltshire - a journey that was to take them over 20 hours, although, owing to War secrecy, none of the recruits knew it at the time. It was to be a long and tedious journey. That first evening and night were particularly laborious, more so because as soon as darkness fell, the black-out curtains were pulled down to prevent light being seen outside. All this was a revelation to the boys who now realised that they were travelling in a country at War. No longer was it magazine stories but stark reality. As the train hissed, coughed and spat under bridges, swished and blasted its way through tunnels, it scared some of the recruits who feared that it could be an enemy attack. When the lights went off, some thought the end had come but this was only done so that the black-out curtains could be lifted and windows opened if necessary. Furthermore, darkness facilitated sleep. While some had travelled on trains before, others had not. The smaller islands never possessed any trains. However, none would have embarked on so lengthy a train journey before. Through the journey the WVS were a constant source of strength and comfort after the protracted travel from home, which now seemed far, far away. Some recruits felt lonely, homesick and vulnerable as they stopped talking, started thinking until sleep, like some potent drug, claimed them.

"Swindon! Swindon!.. This is Swindon!" The announcement, loud and clear, came in a broad West Country drawl. In those days, Swindon used to be a large railway junction where trains stopped for refuelling; the engines were replenished with coal and water. For this reason, the trains carrying the recruits had stopped, causing the boys to awake from their slumber. It was about 8 o'clock in the morning, bright with blue skies and proclaimed all the portents of being a beautiful day.

After refuelling, the train left on the last leg of the journey to Melksham. This should not have taken very long, Swindon being in the same county but rapid progress was impeded by extensive repairs to the tracks, causing the train to crawl at a snail's pace at times, permitting an opportunity for a first view of what many regarded as their Motherland - a most beautiful land as a now sun-drenched day revealed. It was difficult to comprehend that such a complete metamorphosis could have come over the weather in the space of a few hours - from arctic-like conditions to glorious, warm sunshine. The gloom and chagrin of the previous evening in Scotland had vanished to be replaced by smiles all around; words like, 'it's nice man' and 'just like back home' gained currency as opinions, formed on arriving, were hastily being revised. Of course, they could not have known that the weather in the British Isles is renowned for sharp changes - even over a very short time. Another piece of knowledge of which they could not have been aware was that they were travelling South, and that the further South they went, the warmer the weather was likely to become.

As the train progressed - albeit slowly - chugging and screeching, sometimes stopping altogether to facilitate repairs, another wildly held illusion was shattered; another marvel was revealed by the spectacle of women, not men, wielding implements of repair - saws, hammers, wrenches, pickaxes, shovels. The recruits had never before seen white men engaging in this kind of unskilled work - let alone women! They nudged one another in utter disbelief for it was indeed a revelation! Apart from men in the services, most of the white people they had come across in their country at the time had been men in administrations. And yet, although the recruits could not have been aware of it then, they must have been pretty naive because, in the absence of most of the men overseas on War work, someone had to fill the gap in England, though the thought never occurred to them. It was, however, their first eye-opener.

The frequent crawling and stoppages of the troop-train gave the recruits a chance to chat to some of the women through the windows. The women looked tough but were quite friendly and not short of a few words, returning blown kisses and wolf-whistles. They seemed very grateful for the sweets thrown by the young recruits but, more importantly, they particularly welcomed the cigarettes with open arms. A short while later, the train was passing through some of the most beautiful and picturesque countryside ever seen by the boys - different to the rugged, hilly terrain of some of the landscape observed earlier. The recruits could not help being impressed by the orderly, well-arranged hedgerows, the endless, multiplicity of shades of green that criss-crossed to weave delightful and intricate patterns as far as the eye could see.

All the recruits, irrespective of which batch they arrived in, were highly impressed with the beauty of the English countryside as they proceeded to their training camps. The scenery of the landscape made a striking contrast to that in their own countries which, because of the sun, always seemed parched, dry and brown compared to England where everything looked lush and verdant.

The recruits travelling to Melksham duly reached their destination, glad to stretch their legs after such a marathon journey. Because of track repairs, the train had taken some five hours to arrive after leaving Swindon - an unusually long time. The boys looked forward to the short march to the training camp, excited to make assessments of their first footsteps in the Mother Country. Melksham immediately struck one as a sleepy little town, neat, prim and smart in the early spring sunshine. One of the first smells to assault the nostrils was that of growing cabbage and potatoes. The smell was all around and defied escape. People were conspicuous by their absence as the streets seemed deserted. Being a very small town, there would not be many people anyway but the able-bodied men were away on War duty, and the younger women not in one of the forces were away on War work. However, some signs of life were discernible. As the recruits marched along, they could detect the flickering of curtains and sensed that they were being observed from behind them. There was no doubt that those who peered from within did so with a certain amount of trepidation tinged with curiosity. The Westindians marching along might well have been the very first black men they had ever seen and, with only what they had heard and read of these 'people of colour', most of which often was not very flattering, indeed this may have appeared an oddity to behold. For the recruits it felt that all the instincts of those who peered told them that the objects of their stares were not real people but represented objects of fear - savages. An ex-serviceman relives the scene, still alive in his mind after all these years:

> "As we marched along, enjoying the scenery and exchanging our first impressions, we noticed a woman with a little boy clinging to her skirt. The boy looked terrified as, after surreptitiously scrutinizing our posteriors for evidence of tails and hearing me speaking to my friend, shrieked: 'Mummy, Mummy, it speaks!' So we were regarded as inanimate objects and incapable of human utterances. We noticed that the woman made no attempt to admonish the child in any way. Perhaps she was petrified, being a victim of the educational system."

Shortly afterwards the recruits entered the training camp. The reception by way of cuisine that lay in waiting for the new intakes depended on whether they arrived in the earlier batches or in the very final batch.

Pasteur Irons recalls his batch, which arrived at the end of June, 1944, at Filey in Yorkshire, being dined on roast beef, Yorkshire pudding, potatoes and cabbage, followed by a large, green apple each. This, once they had got used to it, was quite substantial as well as appetizing but the boys did not exactly drool over it for, just coming from the Westindies, they would have preferred something a little more appropriate.

George Powe and Gerald Beard, who both arrived in the Autumn of 1944 and who were also at Filey, remember being faced with salad for their first meal. George Powe states:

> "Many of us didn't like it, so we had bread and soup."

And Gerald Beard confesses:

"I just couldn't handle it."

It would appear that the experience gained from the earlier batches of RAF groundcrew recruits served the Air Ministry in good stead and, as a result, the final batch of intakes that went to Melksham benefited accordingly. On entering the RAF camp at Melksham everything looked 'spick and span' and the dining hall, echoing the new spirit of appropriateness, gave the appearance of a five-star hotel bedecked with bright, white tablecloths, ornamented by gleaming knives, forks, spoons and glittering glasses; but what seemed more to the point so far as the newly-arrived recruits were concerned, was the authentic aroma of beef curry and rice. This not only delighted everyone but confounded the predictions of the senior NCO in Trinidad that the boys would not get the kind of food they were accustomed to in England. The boys had not forgotten but were far too busy to care. Their conclusion about the reception - almost to a man - reflected nothing but praise and satisfaction on that occasion and prompted the following recollection:

"Our first meal was like home from home - curry and rice and all our types of foods...well-laid tables, so we were happy. We hardly expected it after what we were told, so it came as a pleasant surprise...."

This VIP-like treatment meted out to this last batch of Westindians was by no means accidental, having almost certainly been instigated by the Colonial Office to whom complaints had been made by representatives of the previous groups.

The Colonial Office was a Civil Service Department with special responsibilities for the colonies and, as such, felt it their bounden duty to look after the interests and welfare of all colonial members of His Majesty's Forces, including the Westindians. For this reason, they had drafted in a certain number of Westindian Aircrew Officers, who had come to the end of their tour of operations, to act as Welfare Officers - an opportunity that presented itself now that the War was nearing its end. The RAF, therefore, through the Colonial Office, now provided for this final intake certain home comforts not available to previous groups - such things as rice, spicy foods, a ration of sugar and extra blankets against the cold nights. For, although it was a mild spring, the lads found the nights rather more than chilly.

So, the new arrivals in the final batch of Westindian groundcrew airmen experienced a very enjoyable first day which was rounded off in the camp's cinema with a welcoming speech by the Commanding Officer followed by a film - 'Shakespeare's Hamlet,' starring a very youthful and somewhat handsome Lawrence Olivier.

The ATS girls from Guyana, Trinidad and Tobago, Barbados, Belize, Jamaica and the smaller Westindian Islands who sailed from America in the Queen Mary for the UK had arrived in August, 1944, at Greenock in Scotland and were now well ensconced in England. From Scotland, the girls - among them Norma Best and Esther Armagon - had travelled by train to London where a tea-party was held for them at which they met the Duke of Devonshire and enjoyed themselves. After a night's rest in the capital, the girls left early the following morning for No. 7 Queen's Camp, Guildford, Surrey, to begin several weeks of rigorous military training.

Also now in Britain was Carol Campbell, the determined Belizian who had paid for her fare to America and from there had herself transported to her destination. Having tried unsuccessfully to join the Women's Auxiliary Air Force (WAAF) as well as the Women's Royal Naval Service (WRNS) she finally enlisted in the ATS and did her initial training in Yorkshire.

BASIC TRAINING CAMPS

The recruits were to spend about two months in basic military training camps. These camps were not solely for Westindians but abounded throughout the length and breadth of the UK for the military preparation of recruits irrespective of their origins. Primarily, the two camps in which Westindians performed their initial military training were Filey in Yorkshire and Melksham in Wiltshire. Those recruits who arrived in the Autumn of 1944, of whom Gerald Beard and George Powe formed a part, found physical exercises in vests and shorts quite a frozen business, although they were constantly being told to 'keep moving' to get the blood circulation going. Such advice to new arrivals from the Caribbean took some believing. According to Gerald Beard:

> "The evenings and nights were the worst. Being built as a holiday camp, Filey had no fireplaces in the billets - only hot pipes - a form of central heating which never seemed to keep us warm."

'Square-bashing' referred to strenuous marches and drills on camp squares, designed to instil discipline and sharp responses to military commands delivered by those who made giving peremptory commands their profession. When executed correctly, drills and marches made an excellent spectacle, slick and smart, which, apart from looking impressive, had the effect of keeping the recruits physically fit, alert and, it was expected, combative; but military training meant much more than 'square-bashing'.

Although all the recruits - irrespective of batch - had quite a lot of military training during the periods they waited to be transported to Britain, the training in which they participated on arrival was, nevertheless, arduous. Stanley Hodges succinctly puts it:

> "At Filey, the real training as servicemen started. 'You're expected to kill or be killed,' our instructors told us."

And Pasteur Irons confirms Stanley Hodges' statement by providing a little more detail:

"We did a lot of physical exercises every day - long runs in, and around the camp's periphery as well as regular cross-country jogs for miles beyond its precincts; and in addition to 'square-bashing', which consisted of marching and drills with or without arms and full packs, we undertook rifle shooting, training in the use of small arms, like revolvers, the manipulation of machine and sub-machine guns plus the usage of many other kinds of weapons. We were taught aircraft recognition - how to distinguish our planes from the Germans' and we had to know all the different kinds of aircraft and weapons used on both sides. We had to master the handling of bayonets, on or off rifles as well as attaining proficiency in the art of unarmed combat."

Training, particularly in the use of weapons such as that described above, was not always given to RAF recruits. This was certainly true of those who joined in the early part of the War. One recalls the Middle East debacle when places like Crete and Tobruk were overrun with heavy casualties because airmen had no idea how to use arms. After that experience every RAF recruit had to undertake initial military training. This was given by members of the RAF Regiment. It was as a result of this episode that large numbers of the Westindian groundcrew staff were introduced into the UK as replacements for those Englishmen sent out to those areas to replace the casualties.

Some of the groundcrew airmen had been allowed to pick the trades they would prefer to work in before arriving in the UK. They were assured that these trades would be available - a fact that influenced some to join. The Westindian recruits at Filey in June, 1944 - among them Stanley Hodges and Pasteur Irons - were not very happy when, on the very first morning of their training, they received the bad news from a Flight Lieutenant Loxton that they would not, after all, be getting the trades they wanted. This caused great resentment and the feeling that they were recruited under false pretences. Many of the boys found themselves in a quandary as to what to do, not having previously thought of a second choice of trade. Pasteur Irons felt so strongly about it that he asked to be sent home. He had the sneaking suspicion that the trades were not really unavailable but were deliberately being withheld from them. In the end some remustered to ACHGD (Aircraft Hand General Duties), while others selected other trades. A few, including Pasteur Irons, remustered to Transport Driving. After the upheaval caused by the unavailability of trades, the real business of initial military training began.

Unlike those recruits that arrived at RAF Melksham Camp which was near enough to the railway station for marching to, the camp at Filey was far enough to permit the use of transport, therefore avoiding immediate contact with the local population. When, at last, the boys did venture into the town some of the locals, apparently scared, distanced themselves with some alacrity. It must, however, be stated that not everyone sought to escape. Some, whether through curiosity or otherwise, were always prepared to stand and pass the time of day. Stanley Hodges mentions how a few people showed them kindness while they were at Filey, and George Powe says:

> "While at Filey when I was off duty I tried to buy things in the shops but I found that I couldn't because they were rationed. Once I walked around and ended up in a pub. I had never been into a pub before, and enjoyed pleasant chats with those inside. Elderly folks visited the camp and invited us to tea parties and other places and we would go round with them to their homes."

Similar benevolence was shown by the locals at Melksham and, indeed, nearly every location at which the boys happened to be stationed. Unpleasant moments did occur, nevertheless there were always those who were prepared to accept the Westindians as they found them, treating them with respect and civility.

The amalgamation of peoples from different Caribbean countries was to form the basis of some conflict among the recruits at Melksham. It must be stressed that, apart from a few minor skirmishes, relations between the recruits of previous batches were mostly harmonious. After all, one would hardly expect total harmony wherever a substantial number of people of varying degrees of temperaments and outlook are assembled. There were several thousands of Westindian RAF groundcrew personnel in the UK and major friction only occurred among the 1500 in the final batch. The general consensus of opinion at the time suggested that this particular conflict was the product of inter-island rivalries and jealousies arising out of insular differences between the Jamaicans on the one hand, and on the other, what they referred to as the "Small

Islanders" - Trinidadians and Tobagans, Barbadians, other islanders and Guyanese - although, Guyana is not an island.

One of the ugliest incidents at Melksham involved fights - not between black and white, but between black and black. A schism developed between Jamaicans and the so-called 'Small Islanders' who were alleged to have found the former somewhat brusque and, to a certain extent, arrogant. There was a similar allegation on the other side, and the fact that there were hot heads on both sides did not help the situation. Anyhow, the two sides became locked in warfare. Using every implement, including, knives, bayonets, buckles, blunt instruments and any weapons they could lay their hands on, they pursued and harassed one another with vehemence whilst hostilities raged. It made a very sad and sorrowful spectacle - blacks fighting blacks in a white man's country. Opinions varied as to what precipitated this fierce internecine confrontation. One theory indicated that it started in the NAAFI, abetted by some individuals on both sides bent on causing trouble, as well as the billetting of the majority of Jamaicans together and having the same arrangement for the 'Small Islanders'. Many felt the seeds of ill-feeling and mistrust had been sewn by the white NCOs when the recruits were at sea by offering what was regarded as preferential treatment to the 'Small Islanders' and telling them uncomplimentary things about the Jamaicans who became highly suspicious. Some of the white NCOs had been with the 'Small Islanders' from the very outset. For instance, they began the journey to the UK with the Guyanese who, on the way, were augmented by the Trinidadians, Barbadians and those from other Islands. These recruits, being first on the ship, procured all the 'plum' jobs such as the preparation and the laying of the tables together with serving as waiters. The Jamaicans, who were always last to be picked up, felt aggrieved when they came on the scene to perform the less attractive ship-jobs.

Matters festered from this point, frictions developed and things came to a head shortly after arriving at Melksham. The catalyst, however, would appear to have been a football match between West Wing, with mostly 'Small-Islanders' and the East Wing, predominantly Jamaicans.

Eric Hudson (Jamaica), Vernon Hunte (Trinidad) and Frank Holder (Guyana) all have vivid memories of the troubles. Eric

Hudson states:

> "Although I didn't go to the football match, I remember that the flare-up started as a result of it, and things began to happen shortly afterwards."

Frank Holder, who attended the match, relives the moment the tinder ignited:

> "From the minute the West Wing scored the winning goal, all hell broke loose. Supporters from both sides charged across the ground attacking the opposition. People were running in all directions; even live rounds were heard. For about two days afterwards things remained tense. Those recruits in the West Wing being situated nearer the NAAFI barred entry to it from the East Wingers who, in turn, denied entry of the West Wingers to the Post Office."

The NAAFI played a very important part in the social life of the camp in the way of drink - both soft and strong - cigarettes, and relaxation; so those to whom entry was barred suffered a distinct disadvantage. Whereas denying entry to the Post Office presented a serious handicap, since, in those first weeks after arrival, vital contacts with home by way of letters, telegrams and money meant a great deal. Yet, with all the upheaval and the violence against the 'opposition', Vernon Hunte, a Trinidadian, says:

> "I survived it all although I was billetted with the Jamaicans. I suffered no ill-effects even at the very height of hostilities - quite remarkable. Apparently, they considered that, living in their quarters, I was one of them."

In the casualty departments of the camp hospital, friends as well as foes discussed this strange 'War,' comparing their wounds and wondering why they were so stupid as to embark upon such a folly. A few individuals attempted to intervene and calm what had become a volatile situation. However, the confrontation was to run its course, lasting for two full days, ending on the third as suddenly as it had begun. One observer, commenting on the termination of hostilities, elucidates:

"I remember feeling a great sense of relief when it was all over, peace abounded and there were handshakes all round, for it was a most shameful episode - and one that should never have happened given cool heads, common sense and spirit of comradeship."

The recruits were to start their basic military training, details of which have been given previously, but this training was further delayed by the visitation of mumps as a form of chastisement for the iniquity of fighting amongst themselves. The thought struck many that they had to make atonement, for no sooner the indiscretion ended, the mumps began. Nearly the entire intake, over 1500 men, were confined to their beds. This affliction was an obvious source of suffering which lasted a fortnight. Yet it was a suffering that provided a great deal of amusement, as Robert Murray reminisces:

"It was very painful - very nasty - especially when it went 'downstairs'. The camp, quite a large one, had one sizeable hospital, which was full, and each dining hall (of which there were at least two) became a hospital for the greater part of 1500 poorly airmen. Anyway, it turned out to be quite a pleasurable occasion for us. The doctors were all women and they used to come around every morning to inspect their patients to see how 'the swelling down there' was getting on. They seemed to have glints in their eyes as they poked and prodded and asked, 'how are you today?' Such a question never failed to evoke a burst of laughter. We used to look forward to it and gave the exercise a military name - 'porting arms for inspection'!"

Fortunately, no fatalities occurred at Melksham as a result of the plague of mumps but Pasteur Irons recollects two Jamaican recruits - Patrick Marshall and Byron Williams - passing away at Filey as a result of meningitis. He went to their funeral at RAF Cemetery, Harrogate and there was a bit of panic afterwards fearing there might have been an epidemic.

However, life in the RAF training camps did not only consist of internecine strifes, unpleasantness, 'square-bashing' and other military training. There were more pleasurable moments recalled by the recruits. When the boys went into the towns, either in Filey or in Melksham, in search of entertainment (which was mostly dancing), relations with the local population were always cool and distant. In the remoter parts of Britain, blacks were often only read about in books, the contents of which were not always favourable. First dances, therefore, didn't come very easily but generally, once the ice was broken and confidence developed, progress came, perhaps slowly at first, then in torrents. Speaking of Melksham, Frank Holder says:

> "The first night we went into the town things were difficult to begin with. Then the boys started to jive amongst themselves and when the girls saw how we moved, one or two threw caution to the wind and began dancing with us. Soon a trickle became a downpour and a downpour became a flood until many of the boys found partners."

So much for the NCO and his prognostications! Other pleasurable periods were passed in friendly banter whilst playing billiards, snooker, football, cricket - one recalls with fondness of going out to start a cricket match at 9 o'clock at night while at Melksham. These memories would remain with the recruits for the rest of their lives as they would never have seen such a phenomenon before:

> "For those were the days of Double Summer Time when there was very little darkness at night, except for a very short period sometime early in the morning. Other than that, there was almost permanent daylight. Mothers would moan that their children couldn't sleep."

The idea of Double Summer Time served the purpose of giving the farmers a greater amount of daylight to grow more food as, during the War, almost everything had to be homegrown. There was also the added advantage that enemy aircraft would be reluctant to participate in raids during daylight. Another cricket enthusiast goes on to elaborate:

> "Starting a limited overs cricket match (say 20 overs) meant that we had ample time to play and complete the match, to the joy and happiness of the boys, many of whom were capable cricketers. To see the sun shining at 11 o'clock at night was a marvel to us. In the Caribbean, darkness always falls around 6pm., and we had just come from there."

TRADE TESTS, TRADE TRAINING, OPERATIONAL DUTIES

On the completion of basic military training, the recruits now became fully-fledged airmen. Each one was then given an assessment examination known as a 'trade test' in order to determine what duty he would perform in the service. George Powe reflects:

> "We had to go through another series of intelligence tests which lasted for about a fortnight, and, on the results of these tests, they told us what trades they felt were appropriate for us."

In fact, there were different types of aptitude tests which fell broadly into three categories - clerical, mechanical and general duties. Those gaining high marks in the mechanical tests found themselves in radar, wireless operating, flight mechanic or technical trades. Those attaining excellent marks in English and maths were allotted jobs in administration, clerical, pay and equipment accounts, etc. The low scorers of marks in all tests became Aircraft Hands General Duties - ACHGD, for short or general 'dog's body'.

The tests described above related essentially to RAF groundcrew. Aircrew servicemen underwent different forms of assessment. Ulric Cross explains:

> "You would then have this exam. This decided whether people would be pilots, navigators and so on. I think everybody who came over with me with one exception, a chap who went to school with me, were navigators. The rest were pilots and went to Canada to train as such. The navigators stayed in Britain."

Hence, the distinction between aircrew and groundcrew was most clearly differentiated as to the training each received.

The aircrew obtained much more specialized training in comparison to the groundcrew, and this would sometimes involve going to Canada; but not every Westindian aircrew recruit was trained in Canada. Many received their training in England, and a large proportion of these, for reasons best left unexplained, could only pass out as Senior NCOs - sergeants rising to flight-sergeants and terminating as warrant Officers, the highest of the non-commissioned ranks. A case in point was that of Godfrey Petgrave who trained in England as a wireless operator/air-gunner, and passed out as a Sergeant, promoted to Flight-Sergeant after one year, then upgraded to the rank of Warrant Officer a year later.

Although not an aircrew member, Godfrey Petgrave was trained in, and knew many aspects of, aircrew work; from the time of passing out, like most aircrew members, he was constantly being transferred to various stations. From ACRC St John's Wood, London, he went to Bridlington, near Filey in Yorkshire where he did his 'square-bashing', then on to ITW (Initial Training Wing) and flying and radio training at Number 4 Radio School, Madeley, Herefordshire. He still recalls his peer group at the time - Bob Murray, Lindo, Charley Atherton, Lee Samms, Ken Wong and many others. Next he was sent to the AFU (Advance Flying Unit) in Wolverhampton on Ansons, then on to OTU, Silverstone on Wellington Bombers, proceeding from there to Bottisford, Nottingham, where he was involved with the Heavy Conversion Unit on Lancaster Bombers before moving on to Bruntisthorpe, Leicestershire.

Like Godfrey Petgrave, Billy Strachan too, trained as a wireless operator/airgunner, also passing out with the rank of sergeant. However, unlike Godfrey Petgrave, Billy Strachan joined a squadron of Wellingtons immediately after completion of his training and found himself thrown into nightly raids over the major German industrial cities:

> "We went to Bremen, Frankfurt, Cologne. We made one trip to Berlin, bombed the battleships Scharnhorst and the Gneisenau, but most of the time we bombed the Ruhr, Germany's industrial heartland."

As one of a very small number of Westindian aircrewmen, Billy Strachan's time in the Royal Air Force was most extra-ordinarily spent in that he underwent training twice. Having survived 30 operations, he was entitled to be given a ground based position.

However, as he puts it: "When asked what I wanted to do, I replied: retrain as a pilot!"

His fervent desire to become an officer came about in a most extra-ordinary manner. One day his white South African Commanding Officer - also his best friend - summoned him, announcing:

> "You have no respect for me or anyone else, so I'm going to recommend you for a promotion." Billy showed immense elation as he reflects. "My training as a pilot began on 'Tiger Moths` taking off at 50 mph, and never going below 75 mph - even a jaguar could easily have overtaken us."

Being young, he learned quickly, being allowed to go solo after just seven hours flying, indulging in pranks, paying unauthorized visits to friends on airfields all over England, finally ending up at Cranwell in Lincolnshire, the RAF Training School for Officers, where he achieved his ambition of flying Wellingtons.

> "Virtually every night we encountered heavy flak. It was 1941, the most desperate time of the war. The Germans had over-run Europe and controlled the whole Atlantic coastline down to the Spanish frontier. Every target was heavily defended. The maximum height at which Wellingtons could fly was 20,000 feet which was well within the range of the German anti-aircraft guns. They continued to fire solidly all the time on the principle that they were bound to hit something.
>
> "As wirelesss operator, I sat with the navigator and pilot while the two gunners sat in their turrets at the front and rear of the plane. The very thick, heavy clothing we wore to counter the cold in those unpressured, unheated cabins, made moving or crouching along turrets to replace a wounded crew-mate extremely difficult."
>
> "We had several narrow escapes. Once, when the navigator, who was also the bomb-aimer, was lying flat on his back looking down the aimer, a bullet flew over his head, under the pilot's backside and up the side of my leg - I still have the scar to prove it. Yet, I was never terrified. In fact, none of us was. I suppose we had the over-confidence of youth. We never thought it would happen to us. We were a tight unit - as a crew we did everything together. We came back, had parties, checked up to see who were lost and heartlessly said things like - "Oh, I'll have his bike."

At Cranwell Air Training School, Billy had his first 'batman.` He was a real, smooth, Jeeves type who had been 'batman' to George VI: "I was a little 'coloured boy' from the Caribbean and I instinctively called him, Sir."

"No sir," he hastily corrected "It's I who call you sir." Billy broke his hip when performing acrobatics in training. He also had his face operated on at Ely hospital, and just as he became a fully fledged bomber pilot, the RAF switched from his favourite Wellingtons to Sterlings. "They were death-traps," he recalls with a shudder.

Billy was to crash again while on a practice raid, enduring another spell in hospital, after which he joined a squadron of Lancasters at Swinderby, Lincolnshire.

Neither was training for aircrews restricted to England and Canada. Owen Sylvester, a Trinidadian who joined the RAF in 1941 and holder of the Distinguished Flying Medal (DFM), found himself being allocated to three venues to do his initial training, the first two of which turned out to be unsuitable for political reasons. This happened to be South Africa, which, with the best will in the world, could hardly have been described as appropriate - even though it was then part of the British Commonwealth. A similar mistake was made with regard to the next training venue chosen for Owen Sylvester - a place called Pensacola in the USA which, although war allies of Great Britain, enacted similar racial policies as South Africa. In both cases the RAF hierarchy had to effect change with alacrity. In the end, Owen Sylvester was sent to Canada for his training.

There was very little contact given between the groundcrew and aircrew for mainly two reasons. Firstly, most aircrew airmen joined in the early part of the War, whereas, the first batch of groundcrew did not join until mid-1943, arriving in Britain in 1944. Secondly, unless the groundcrew airmen worked on aircrafts or allied trades such as flight mechanic, aircraft finishers or radar, the two hardly ever came into contact. Ulric Cross, one of the highest ranked and decorated of all Westindians - being a Squadron Leader, DFC/DSO and Bar, puts the matter in perspective when he says:

> "To a very large extent most aircrew had been cut off from the rest of the Westindians. It would merely be by accident that there were a couple of Westindians on the station as groundcrew. When you are flying, apart from the groundcrew who dealt directly with airplanes that you were

flying, you had very little contact with groundcrew. This was not true certainly of the other services of the Army or Navy but it was certainly true of the Air Force, where, if you were aircrew, your only other contact was with members of your crew in the aircraft, and you built up a sort of relationship, a very close relationship, obviously with these people. I was in a crew of only two, a pilot and a navigator. So far as the aircrew was concerned, your contact was with the people who looked after the airplane, the engineers, mechanics and so on. You built up a relationship with them. Also you were, to an extent, isolated from the rest of the RAF. In the sense that you were an officer, as such, you only met other officers ..... It was not easy to build up relationships with groundcrew Westindians. In fact, there could have been other aircrew officers on the station (if it was a large station) whom you'd never seen."

The groundcrew servicemen were generally given no choice as to their allotted duties despite the 'trade tests'. George Powe's account illustrates the experiences of some individuals:

"I was told that I could have a number of choices. I could do radar, join the technical branch, wireless operating or flying if I liked. But the service was so structured that they wanted mostly radar people at the time. I was in that category so I had no choice but to do radar. Having been told what the choices were, you were then allocated to what was available."

The harvested yield of servicemen from the Caribbean was distributed all over the United Kingdom. Many expected to be sent further afield but, with few exceptions, they were disappointed. A European, African or Asian posting might not have displeased some but the stock answer was always the same: 'you're already overseas'. One groundcrew airman recollects being sent to Ghent in Belgium only to be recalled as soon as he arrived. The reason for the urgent recall signal? A posting error had been made. However, a very small number did get through the net. Such a person was Adrian Nrysnich, a Jamaican, who trained as an engineer at Low Moor, Lancaster before being posted to Ismailia in Egypt, where he underwent further training, and found himself close to the battlefield - something that, when he left his native Jamaica, he never thought would have been his lot. Yet, having volunteered, he accepted the situation and felt resigned to whatever fate awaited him. His job was to repair the engines and send them to the front. He admits:

> "I could feel the War in my bones. I said to myself, 'well, this is it'. I didn't believe I would return to Jamaica."

Stanley Hodge's original trade in the RAF as indicated by his trade test was to be an unpleasant experience. His trade, that of an aircraft finisher, required that he should repair and refurbish the aircraft, both interior and exterior but the materials used in this task, in conjunction with the weather, had an adverse affect on his health, causing him to be hospitalised for some time. Upon being discharged from hospital, he changed his trade to that of a motor transport driver (MTD).

Athleston Holder was posted to a camp called Madeley in Herefordshire where he worked in the bicycle stores and was in charge of the games room. His perception at the time of the work allotted to Westindians represented the popular view held by some of them when he reflects:

> "They would give us ACHGDs all the skivvy work like sweeping up and cleaning lavatories. The next big group performed motor driving duties and motor mechanic, few did clerical work; only a very small minority of Westindian groundcrew airmen found themselves in the technical field."

As previously mentioned, some servicemen, like Pasteur Irons, felt they were not being allotted to the trades earmarked for them. In Pasteur Iron's case his protestations led to his being posted to a number of different camps. First, he went to a Maintenance Unit at Filton, Bristol, where his duties included some engineering and mechanical training for six weeks. From there he was transferred to Blackpool Motor Training Section where dissatisfaction still possessed him. He felt that the training still failed to live up to what was promised, and, after further remonstrations, he found himself once more on the move, this time bound for RAF Skellingthorpe in Lincolnshire, doing repairs and fittings on Lancaster Bombers. Here his wanderings came to an end, for he never moved again until the war ended.

But not every RAF Westindian groundcrew airman failed to obtain the trade he wanted. Indeed, they were represented in most trades on the ground of which there were many - flight-mechanics, wireless operators, radar, engineers, aircraft finishers, clerical (which included administration) pay and equipment accounts, medical orderlies, motor transport drivers and many others.

George Haynes, who did his initial military training at Melksham, took mechanics and passed out as an air craftman, First Class. He was afterwards posted to RAF Belton Park, Grantham, where he distinguished himself for two years, guarding aeroplanes and ammunition, before being transferred to Catterick, working on and guarding Lancaster Bombers.

George Powe states that he was one of only five individuals out of a total of five hundred stationed at Yatesbury in Wiltshire who specifically trained as radar operators:

> "After completing training at Yatesbury, I went to Penzance in Cornwall to watch the South Coast. My job was to monitor and give directions to Fighter Pilots when they were attacking. That was my assignment. I was there for one year and afterwards I became attached to 78 Fighter Command, West Prawle, South Devon."

In keeping with the very high marks obtained in his trade test, and in order to capitalize on his own abilities, Robert Murray became one of the few Westindian groundcrew airmen to attain Senior NCO rank in only five months from the date of arriving in Britain. It was approaching the end of the War and the authorities felt that thousands of servicemen and women would soon be entering 'Civvy Street' without any basic qualifications. It was therefore decided to provide two formal qualifications - The War Educational and the Forces Preliminary Certificates. Details of intensive courses for potential instructors were circulated throughout the three services. Instructors - people with the necessary qualifications, Junior or Senior Cambridge, London Matriculation or their equivalents - were invited to apply. Robert Murray, armed with the requisite requirements, applied, went on the course and emerged successful in August, 1945, having only arrived in March of that year. He reflects:

> "I became the envy of all - whites as well as blacks. Whites moaned because they claimed they had joined up at the beginning of the War and had gained little or no promotion; and blacks just moaned for the shear hell of it. Yet, the opportunities had been open to everyone. I became an Educational and Vocational Tutor (EVT)."

Gerry Smith's trade test qualifications took him to Coastal Command on flight control duties in the Meteorological Section of a camp not far from Portsmouth. He says:

> "I was there for two years and thoroughly enjoyed myself. There were only ten Westindians on the camp and there was never any trouble. I always found that when we were in small numbers trouble hardly ever occurred. Being a good organist as well as a churchman, I became assistant on the camp and, when the organist was posted, I replaced him for the Church of England. I remember playing at ceremonies and at funerals - particularly on sad occasions when planes were shot down or crashed as sometimes happened."

Ivor De'Souza and Ulric Cross were both part of the aircrew division of the RAF Ivor De'Souza joined in 1940, did the first half of his training in England and completed it in Canada. He became a pilot, reaching the rank of Flight-Lieutenant. His operational posting with an Australian Squadron was as a Flight Commander, being in complete charge of a squadron of twelve aircraft, participating in several 'dog-fights'. He relates:

> "The British instituted a system in which every Commonwealth Squadron - that is, Australian, New Zealand, Canadian or South African - had to consist of at least one RAF crew member. So one can imagine the consternation and leg-pulling when the Australians saw me, a Westindian, for the first time as their Flight Commander!"

Much humour abounded. Jokes were made and taken in the spirit in which they were intended, and Ivor De'Souza thoroughly enjoyed the company of the Australians, passing some pleasant and hilarious times with them.

But, as in life generally, things in the RAF were not always rosy, even for aircrew members. Owen Sylvester, a Warrant Officer and Captain of his crew, could never forget the time when he was made to enter and re-enter the Commanding Officer's office several times on the pretext of his incorrect saluting. The Warrant Officer had just arrived on the station and was in the act of introducing himself, as well as his crew, who were standing outside, when he formed the opinion that the CO took an instant dislike to him. The CO satisfied himself that the saluting was in order and, when the crew lined up before him, he said to the Navigator, who was white, "I suppose, you're the Captain". When the Navigator answered in the negative and indicated the Warrant Officer, the CO seemed not to be amused! He was later overheard to remark:

> "I know how to deal with these people. I have experience of dealing with them in India."

Both Sylvester and his crew, who had every confidence in him, concluded that their future operations would not be easy. Owen Sylvester gritted his teeth and decided to show the CO and his Squadron that he was as good as they were:

> "My crew - all whites - respected and trusted me completely."

In contrast to Ivor De'Souza, Ulric Cross trained in Britain as a navigator at Eastbourne Service Elementary Air Observers School. From there he went to RAF Cranwell, Lincolnshire, for fourteen weeks training in the use of radio, and then proceeded to Scotland to complete his training. This period of training lasted for one year after which an examination and an interview followed. He explains the purpose of the interview;

> "There was nobody in an aeroplane lower than the rank of Sergeant and the interviews were held annually to determine whether you would be a Sergeant or an Officer. If you were a Sergeant, you became the lowest rank after the Pilot Officer, or the Co-Pilot. You didn't necessarily have to be a Pilot in the RAF. You could be a Stores Officer. It was just another rank."

From the above account given by Ulric Cross, it is clear that the aircrew members enjoyed different treatment to those of the groundcrew. Not only did a formal apparatus exist by which they gained promotion, there was also a stipulation on the number of flight operations that a member of the aircrew was permitted to perform. His comments below emphasise this:

> "I was coming off flying. I had done, I suppose, what would generally be regarded as my full quota of operations without a rest. In other words, I

had done eighty operational flights - mainly over Germany. It was quite obvious that, according to rules, I would have to come off flying fairly soon. So, shortly afterwards, it was decided that I should come off."

After completing the specified number of operational flights, Ulric Cross was transferred to the Colonial Office which, though not a new department, was in an embryonic stage of development with only two other staff members in it. He recalls the initial role he was to perform in the department:

"I came off flying operations at the end of November 1944, and went to the Colonial Office as a liaison officer, originally to liaise between the Colonial Office and the Royal Air Force. Eventually my remit was extended to include virtually all colonials in all the services."

During the War the Empire still existed. Britain had a vast number of colonies, peopled by what were described as 'British Subjects'. Dealing with the colonies was the responsibility of the government department known as 'The Colonial Office'. With a substantial number of Westindians and other colonials in the UK at the time, either in the forces or engaged in other War work of some kind, the role of this department was extended. Many of the Westindian officers, having completed their tour of operations, and with the War virtually over, were assigned to the Colonial Office to serve in a welfare and advisory capacity. The Colonial Office was situated in very close proximity to Trafalgar Square, London, but later moved to Victoria Street.

Ivor De'Souza was also recruited into the Colonial Office. In summing up the prospects of entering this department, he states:

"My first reaction when asked to go to the Colonial Office was 'No!', because I was enjoying flying which did not expose me to anything disastrous, except my own stupidity. However in the end I went and had a look, then I saw guys like Ulric Cross, Johnny Spence, Neville Glenbartin, Johnny Johnson and Dudley Thompson. Ulric Cross was the most distinguished Westindian aircrew member of the War. He was in charge of the thing, so I stopped at the Colonial Office".

The objectives and the purpose of the Colonial Office, as it applied to the servicemen and War workers, were not clearly defined, yet Ulric

Cross preferred to opt for what was an ambiguous role in a newly created unit rather than selecting other choices presented to him. In defending his decision to choose the position, he states:

> "I had no particular desire to instruct which was the normal thing that one, after coming off flying, would do. One would go to an RAF school and instruct. Apart from this I think the necessity for instructors was patently becoming less and less since the War was going to end fairly quickly."

The first discernible objective for the Colonial Office Ulric Cross perceived to be, was:

> "....to assist the majority of Westindian aircrew in adjusting to conditions in English civilian life, and also to educate the English about the Westindians."

He goes on to state that:

> "What it was at the beginning was a welfare unit, to liaise and assist in settlement and try to solve the problems that arose because of an influx of a large number of Westindians in the British services - particularly the RAF groundcrew."

This required him to do a lot of defending of Westindians who faced court martial charges. This defending, he maintains, consisted, to a large extent, of explaining different customs, habits of thought, modes of behaviour of Westindians to the English people. He continues:

> "....For example, there was a large unit in Buckinghamshire. I had to go out to them in response to questions which arose from a telephone message. There were always problems either about food, discipline or something at the unit and I would go and find out what it was all about. You had two things: one - Westindians that had no tradition of service in Armed Forces and had problems in adjusting to that; secondly - the English, who had no experience of dealing with Westindians, generally had their problems. Our function really was to try to explain each side's point of view to the other, in a sense."

However, the major difficulty, which was to present itself frequently when speaking to the groundcrew, was that they actually saw their relations with people outside as the most problematic thing. This for Ulric Cross necessitated that the Colonial Office attempted to see "the problem from the point of view of everybody". With this remit in mind, the Colonial Office was essentially perceived as the beginning of a race relations unit.

There also existed another function to which the Colonial Office had to apply itself:

> "There was another angle to the unit, certainly when I came off flying in 1944, which was after D-day in June. I came off flying in November and it was quite obvious that the War would be ended fairly soon. The question of the resettlement and the repatriation of thousands would arise. So the unit which originally started as a welfare unit for colonial staff, was expanded to include all the people from the colonies in all the services, and was eventually converted into a resettlement unit."

Westindian individuals who were not in the Armed Forces and had come to Britain to work in the factories feared that they would be forced to fight. Dudley Miller recalls going to Low Moor, Lancaster, where confrontation instantly arose. The Westindians were told that they had to be trained in the use of weapons, rifles, bayonets, machine-guns, etc., as well as learning military drill. This confirmed their worst fears, that they were going to be forced into the army to fight, the very thing they didn't want to do. There was a big rumpus because the Westindian's in this case were assured before leaving Jamaica that they would be working in factories. Such was the ferocity of the complaints that the Jamaican government became involved and sent a representative to explain the situation to the workers. They were told that they were in war conditions and that they must obey orders. They were further assured that they would not be forced to fight but they had to be trained in the use of weapons and had to accept the discipline for the sole reason of protecting themselves. If the Nazis invaded Britain every member of the military and non-military forces, especially those working on ammunition, would be expected to defend themselves and the country. It was further pointed out that if the Nazis won the War, Britain, the Commonwealth and Jamaica, would perish. After that, there was no further trouble.

EXPERIENCES ON CAMP

It has long been long suspected and to some degree supported, by psychological theory, that co-operation, camaraderie, friendship and good feelings are fostered by individuals united in the pursuit of a common goal and against a common aggressor. On this basis one would expect little conflict to exist on the camps where Westindian servicemen performed their duties to defeat the Nazis. The experience of the aircrew servicemen seems to have been in accordance with this reasoning, as depicted by Ulric Cross's and Ivor De'Souza's experiences on their operational camps, in that they experienced little or no conflict as a result of their colour. One of Ulric Cross's recollections, which confirms this 'cohesion and togetherness', he felt, was when on one occasion he was lent £1 by a South African pilot to buy a drink in the pub. One must bear in mind that, although apartheid had not been put on the statute books until the National Party was given a mandate in the 1948 election, since 1910 racial discrimination had been institutionalised in South Africa. Hence, the significance of this incident for Ulric Cross qualified his perception of harmony in the forces and that colour or race had not been a problem while he was in the RAF. He goes on to state emphatically:

> "No! No! I was best man at the wedding of two of the chaps from my Squadron. I'm going down some time this month to spend the weekend with my first pilot and my last pilot, who incidentally live five miles of each other in East Devon."

Ivor De'Souza recalls having a "lovely time" on his camp with the Australian Squadron to which he was attached. He recalls being sent parcels of fruit cake from Australia. That was a "tremendous comfort" to him, and, in an affectionate manner, the way he and his comrades relaxed and amused themselves when not on operational duties accorded him great satisfaction:

> "We played violent games. We would turn a cushion into a rugby ball and play rugby, and you know, if anyone got hurt, no one would worry

about you. Some people got ever so tense, naturally, but it was all great fun. You had to let off steam in all kinds of ways, things like two chaps holding you upside down so that your feet got boot polished. If you were on unpopular terms for some reason then they pulled your trousers down, daubed your backside with the polish and put your backside's print on the floor. This was just another way of letting off steam."

Similarly, Billy Strachan, the Jamaican, even as a wireless operator/air-gunner, and prior to bcoming an officer - experienced little or no difficulty by way of discrimination when he says:

"If by any reasonable calculation, one might have expected me to have suffered, if not discrimination, at least a constant barrage of racist jokes, I can confirm that this did not happen. In fact, so-far as I can remember, never was I looked at askance because of my colour."

However, another aircrewman paints a quite different picture:

"I was an aircrew member and, believe me, there was prejudice and discrimination - albeit covert but one took no notice of it. I'm sure that those trained in Canada struck it lucky as most passed out as officers, whereas most of those trained in England could only achieve the higher non-commissioned ranks."

Therefore, for Ulric Cross, Ivor De'Souza and others there was little animosity as a consequence of their being Westindians. This had been the experience of nearly all the aircrew officers. For the majority of the groundcrew the tales they were to tell echoed the accounts given by the anonymous air serviceman. Athleston Holder recalls being treated "quite badly" and confronting a lot of racial prejudice. A familiar experience that he, and others, encountered was constantly being questioned about their presence in Britain. The implications behind such questions were not difficult to decipher:

".... you got asked constantly, 'why leave a warm sunny country to come to a dark, cold, England?'. We felt our presence wasn't really welcomed. The questions were not always asked with the best intentions."

Robert Murray's standard reply to such questions was always:

"We can't eat the sun."

Gerald Beard's experience of racism on his operational camp was initiated by the American servicemen who were stationed with him:

"....they seemed to think themselves superior, more or less. Well, they weren't in my section. As far as I was concerned, I saw them and passed them, but some of them expected you to salute them or things like that. One pulled me up once telling me that he was an officer. I said, 'well, I don't know nothing about you, pal.' He was in a different section altogether, so I told him to 'buzz off', so that was it!"

This conflict was essentially between Westindians and white American soldiers. This seemed contrary to the friendliness and affable relations that most of the Westindian recruits experienced on the journey to Britain. However, unlike the relationship they had with white Americans, Gerald Beard and Robert Murray recall that the Westindians developed good relationships with the African-Americans.

Robert Murray recounts one event and the conversation he had with a group of African-American servicemen. He, along with these Americans, were being taken for a tour around London by taxi. He recalls the companionship between these individuals from different spheres of the world, with the Americans being very "courteous as well as generous, treating him to whatever they had to eat and drink without payment." He goes on to relate:

"....being very excited when the taxi-driver announced, 'We're now under the River Thames, boys'. This was a source of great amazement to me. As we were being driven, the conversation ranged over a wide field of topics, politics being mostly dominant. All the African-Americans were resolute about not returning home to the conditions that prevailed before the War; 'No sir,' they'd say, 'we ain't gonna stand for it. There's gonna be a whole lot-a trouble'. And so there was in the 1950s and 1960s."

Gerald Beard recalls the Westindian airmen developing such good relationships with the African-Americans to the extent that:

"..... we had to back them up several times. Some of them, I don't know

87

if it's because, more or less, they were used to the American way of treatment, subordinated themselves, you know."

Ulric Cross speculates as to why the groundcrew Westindians experienced an opposite relationship with their white fellow servicemen to that of the aircrew members when he states:

"I think that there were two reasons. I don't know if this is true but as an officer you were obviously meeting people who were of a higher standard of education, than the average population. Secondly, you were meeting people of this standard of education, and also who couldn't look down on you, because, very often, you had the same or a higher standard of education. So it would be very difficult, I would imagine, for them to look down on a black man in such circumstances."

However, intellectual ability or, indeed, professional expertise, even when in the aircrew division, at the end of the day was less instrumental in enhancing one's progress through the ranks than other factors sometimes proved to be. Ronald Hall, a Guyanese who joined the RAF in 1941 attached to the aircrew section and passed out as a Sergeant Navigator, exemplifies this point perfectly. Stationed in Tunisia, a circular came around asking if anyone spoke French. He answered the request and was made Education Officer, teaching French. Then, in Italy, he found his excellent knowledge of Latin fitted him out admirably to learn Italian, the two languages being closely allied. By procuring a book on the rudiments of Italian and by conversing with as many of the natives as possible - particularly the women - he became quite proficient at the language. Even Italians were sometimes surprisingly, shocked at this "black man" who spoke English, French and Italian. It was whilst chatting to an Italian female laundry worker that his CO, a Squadron Leader Beale, asked him where the nearest laundry was, information which Hall easily extracted from the laundry worker, and offered to accompany his CO there, an offer which received acceptance. Whilst at the laundry, Hall showed his value once more through his understanding of Italian and interpreting for his CO.

Seeing his Commanding Officer being grossly overcharged, Hall intervened to reveal the intended 'robbery' to the utter annoyance of the Italian, now babbling away and waving his arms about frantically, no doubt regretting having to receive the equivalent of fifteen pounds instead of the near one hundred pounds he had in mind. This profitable saving by Squadron Leader Beale, coupled with Hall's facility with languages - as a Sergeant - having already been popular amongst the officers for saving them pounds purchasing their wines and spirits, he found himself in front of his Group Captain at the end of his thirty-ninth operation. The Group Captain could not contain his admiration for Hall's talents, questioning him about his background, parentage, education etc., At the end of the interview, the Group Captain informed Hall he was going to give him a commission. Hall received the information with surprise as he was the first to be commissioned in the field after only thirty-nine operations. The Group Captain then asked Hall where he would like to go. He could go to Egypt where most of his friends were but he opted for England instead and soon found himself at a camp in Gloucestershire where, two weeks after arriving, his new Commanding Officer summoned him, told him to take a week's leave and gave him a voucher to obtain an officer's uniform. He now became a Pilot Officer. Six months later he was promoted to Flying Officer, with a final promotion to Flight Lieutenant shortly afterwards - all of which had nothing to do with his flying.

However, your intellectual ability, or indeed professional expertise, even when in the aircrew division, at the end of the day was no guarantee of your progress through the ranks. Certainly other factors proved to be instrumental, at times, in gaining promotion if you were a black man. Ulric Cross tells about his first promotion:

"As it happened, and I don't know to what extent my getting commissioned was influenced by these two factors, but as it happened, the day before the interviews, the whole navigation school was closed down and everybody, pupils and instructors, went on a six mile cross - country race in Scotland and I happened to win it. The next day I was interviewed and as far as I can remember, there were only two matters that came up at the interview. I walked into the interview room and the first thing the Group Captain said was 'congratulations on a splendid race yesterday, Cross'. The next one was, 'do you know Leary Constantine?' and it so happened that I did. To what extent these were responsible for getting a commission I don't know but I know I was commissioned an officer shortly afterwards."

Hence the stereotype that existed concerning black people possibly had a positive influence on Ulric Cross becoming an officer. In contrast, being black was a hindrance for Stanley Hodges. Working as a motor transport driver with five other black MTDs, he instances an experience:

> "We noticed that we only seemed to get the menial duties, like the coal wagon, the runway sweeping and so on, never one of the outgoing long distance jobs. We thought this wasn't good enough so we decided to make a formal complaint ...... We also complained to the CO about the lack of promotion among us because it was obvious to us our white companions, including the WAAF drivers, were being promoted and we were overlooked."

This complaint was to receive a favourable and prompt response from the Commanding Officer on behalf of the black servicemen, and within six months all six black MTDs were promoted. Nevertheless, other than this incident, there was no preferential treatment experienced by the servicemen with the exception of the food that was made accessible to them. George Powe confirms:

> "...we were treated like any other servicemen except that, in one camp, they tended to give us our own food, like rice and milk and all this kind of thing. Something more fitting other than what they termed Westindian food but, apart from that, nothing."

In keeping with the statement attributed to Napoleon that "an army marches on its stomach", overall food remained readily available to the servicemen, although this food at times was not the type Westindians necessarily ate but, given time, one gets used to anything, and, with the passage of time, the Westindians grew accustomed to the English cuisine. Hence, the experience of the servicemen while in their operational camps revealed that they were generally well catered for in respect of the food they received. In fact the family of James Moore fared better in the War, which illustrates the extent of prejudice and racism that he and his family experienced in Britain before the War began. As his daughter recalls:

> "In one sense, family life did improve significantly during the War... With my father back in the army and mother getting a little allowance

plus being able to go to work, we were now almost well off! She picked up a job because there were more jobs going for women. We were at school, so that little money and everything helped and we had those little extras that we never had before.... I only remember one really good Christmas and things came from friends where my mother was working and that was during the War. People sent lots of gifts for us but previously to that, on a Christmas morning, we just had an apple and orange with a couple of biscuits .... Prejudice didn't really die down during the War. It was just that the War took up most of people's time."

With the majority of Westindian servicemen being groundcrew, few actually had any warfare experience. In fact Stanley Hodges argues that the action that most groundcrew had to face occurred between themselves and fellow white RAF servicemen:

"....there were skirmishes at almost every camp where black people were stationed."

However, Stanley Hodges does recall one incident where his camp was attacked by the Nazis:

"The camp was under bomber command, a camp from which the bombers operated night-time bombing raids over Germany. I can remember one particular night after the bombers had dropped their bombs on Germany and were returning to base ..... German fighter-bombers followed them at high altitude unknown to English and Canadian crews. When the bombers were about to land the German fighter-bombers opened up with machine-gun fire....... two Canadians were killed and I witnessed two or three bombers destroyed."

Ulric Cross and Ivor De'Souza, like all aircrewmen, certainly experienced more combat action than some of their compatriots. Ulric Cross, being a navigator, recalls his main operational duty being to bomb Berlin. This tour of duty used to be termed by individuals the "Berlin milk run". Such was the regularity and ferocity with which the airmen carried out their duty that Ivor De'Souza referred to these bombing raids as delivering to "clients". He goes on to describe his missions:

"We started doing low level day-flights, bombing railways and workshops. I think the first one I did was in Germany. It was low level, right down, I mean low, fifty feet. It became rather expensive, too many people had been shot down. Then we went to a different force and instead of dropping bombs you were dropping coloured markers for the heavies coming behind to bomb."

Ulric Cross survived seven crashes, none of which seriously hospitalised him or prevented him from carrying out his operational duties, which he performed from March 1943 to November 1944.

Nevertheless, Ulric Cross's seven crashes and miraculous escapes happened to many others during the War. The line between death and survival seemed very thin then and very few, being in the flush of youth, had either the inclination or the time to think of such things. Ever since that ill-fated first meeting of Owen Sylvester and his new Commanding Officer, both he and his crew felt convinced that he was out to "destroy" them. Yet, the thought could only have been a fleeting one for all, Operational Aircrew Members during the War lived a 'temporary existence'. All such flights carried an element of danger! Owen Sylvester reminisces:

"The idea of getting into action was paramount in my mind - and no-one could have deflected me from that resolve. One felt responsibility for one's crew, one went into each OP with a sense of doing a job that had to be done! When a job was planned, one went to the 'Briefing Room' and was briefed about the defences of the enemy and the route to be followed. My aircraft was the Lancaster Bomber. One had to wait for hours, this was the time one's briefing took place. In the North Pole the sky overhead got dark. One felt a sense of 'Twilight'. Things did not appear real.

We had to fly our aircraft over enemy territory under their radar system, once I remember seeing their 'tracer bullets' coming up. One saw all sorts of different colours! One saw no danger in this although it was obviously dangerous. All the guns were synchronized. If you didn't get out of that then you were lost -and could well be shot down! We were going over Stuttgart when, suddenly, I was caught in a 'Stall'. I can't remember what I did, but I was falling through the sky. From 22,000 feet I found myself at about 9,000 feet in what seemed like seconds. The bomb-aimer was put on his tummy, I got caught in the massive searchlights and I had to take evasive action hastily! The altimeter was whizzing around at an enormous rate; everything seemed to be flying past me and sticking to the ceiling. It was the only time in my operation I thought I was done for. There wasn't enough time. Owing to gravity, I wasn't in any position to do anything. I saw one of my friend's aircraft go down but I was so busy with my own difficulties, I had no time to say 'God, bless his soul'. In desperation I had to get the engineer to pull the joy stick back; fortunately for me and my crew it worked. I began to level out and gradually regained height, it's only when I levelled out that I realised what I'd done. I had no sense of fear, only my sense of duty and my training caused me to escape! Only years after the War such things struck me as dangerous and heroic. It was such a wonderful experience that one never thought of heroics at the time, I felt a sense of elation - although I could not say why!"

Ivor De'Souza relates his story:

"We were expected to keep an aircraft over the whole of the railway line, going back and forth between Munster and Osnaburg and, if anything moved, we had it straight away."

He goes on to state that he and others in the Squadron could sense D-day approaching and were called upon to go on reconnaissance flights to detect whether the Nazis were doing anything suspicious. When D-day occurred on the 6 of June, 1944, Ivor De'Souza was in a prime seat to see the beginning of the allied invasion of Europe. He recalls this large-scale operation vividly:

"We had this remarkable sight coming back over our heads. We saw these coloured lights in the sky approaching us and we thought, 'What's this?' Of course these were the bombers towing the gliders and we had this feeling then that we were witnessing the beginning of the end of the War."

Billy Strachan's first operation as a pilot officer featured a day-light raid over Nordhausen, recorded, like all his other operations, in his log-book in blue ink for day raids, and in red ink for night raids. These raids were incessant, sleep being short and the dangers, horrifying. Every trick in the book came into play. Billy became famous for his hair-raising, but brilliant practice of evading German fighters. The trick was to wait until the enemy were right on his tail and, at the last minute, he would cut the engines entirely sending his lumbering Lancaster into a plunging dive, letting the fighters overshoot harmlessly above.

"Bombers," recalls Billy, "were big, heavy, trundling things.

Fighters had heavier cannons with longer range than us and they were of course much faster and more manoeuvrable. The ME-110, a turn-engine night-fighter, always attacked from above and the rear. The moment they came diving at you, you cut the engines."

It was not until his 15th trip as a bomber pilot that Billy finally lost his nerve - which, once lost, he never regained:

> "I remember so clearly. I was carrying a 12,000 pound bomb destined for some German shipping. We were stationed in Lincolnshire and our flight-path was over Lincoln Cathedral.
>
> The city of Lincoln stands on a hill, so you took off below the level of the cathedral - you had to take very great care to avoid the spire, climbing quite quickly to get over the top of it. This meant tricky work at the best of times, and with a huge bomb like the one I was carrying that night, I could only expect to clear the top of the spire narrowly.
>
> It was a foggy night, with visiblity being about 100 yards. I asked my engineer, who stood beside me to make sure we were on course to get over the top. He replied: "We're just passed it." I looked out and suddenly realized that it was just beyond our wing-tips, to the side. It was sheer luck. I hadn't seen it at all - and I was the pilot! There and then my nerve went. I realized I simply couldn't go on. This was the last straw. I knew it was the end of me as a pilot. I flew to a special 'hole' we had in the North Sea where no allied shipping ever went near and dropped my 'big one.' Then I flew back to the airfield."

But if the impression has been given that life in the RAF for the Westindians consisted of nothing other than strife, moans, groans and dissatisfaction, one must hasten to dispel such views for nothing could be further from the truth. Strife, fights and dissatisfaction certainly existed and more will be said about this later, but they did not occur to the exclusion of everything else.

The service people spent many pleasurable hours indulging in their favourite pastimes, which were wide and varied. In athletics, the names of Arthur Wint and E. MacDonald-Bailey come automatically to mind but dozens more indulged in the sport. In the field of entertainment, many took their first faltering steps whilst still in the RAF, which provided the stage for the parading of their latent talents and a few amongst them, Nadia Katouse, Frank Holder and Cyril (CY) Grant - all of whom became fully accomplished artistes - prospered.

Then there was cricket, at which many of the boys excelled.

Almost every sizeable RAF station had its fair complement of Westindian cricketers, bowlers, batsmen, wicket-keepers, and the hierarchies of these stations were rightly proud of some of their more outstanding Westindian cricketers, many of whom often reflected that their best times in the Royal Air Force were spent on the cricket field. One benefited considerably in the services if one was sports-orientated and good at it! Cricket, that bat and ball game the English took to the Westindies and taught to the natives, became their way of life, their religion, and this way of life continued in England even though a War was on. Robert Murray could never forget the day he asked to be released from section duty to play a cricket match for the station. He was told in no uncertain manner to keep working: "There is a war on". A few minutes later the telephone rang and he answered it. The station's Adjutant, who was the Captain, bellowed: "Murray, why the hell aren't you on the coach?!"

When told the Flight Sergeant wouldn't release him, the Adjutant snapped: "Put him on." Immediately the Flight Sergeant turned from the telephone and ordered Robert Murray: "Drop everything and run!" Ever since that day the first question every morning was: "Any cricket today?"

And in the cricket match, fired by Robert Murray's quick three wickets, his Captain promised to give him a £1 note, a phenomenal sum at the time, if he bagged the opposition Captain's wicket, also a station's Adjutant. Obviously there was great professional jealousy. He was a fine attacking batsman, and in no time had scored 25 sparkling runs but, according to Robert Murray's Captain: "he is a cocky bastard!". Shortly afterwards, Robert Murray produced probably the best ball of his life, a fast Yorker, right up in the block hole, shattering the stumps to the utter ecstasy of his Captain. The Captain presented him with the promised £1 note in addition to an exaggerated hug, overjoyed to be victorious in the match, and thrilled to "put one over his cocky rival". Needless to mention, the beer flowed like water after the match. Cricket was, and still is, one of the common loves of both black Westindians and white British. Some of the ex-servicemen used this shared love of cricket as a means of developing mutual respect and understanding between the peoples of the Caribbean and Britain.

The Westindian women - predominantly ATS - who did their

basic training at No. 7 Queens Camp, Guildford, Surrey, were now widely dispersed throughout the UK, torn asunder from their closely-knitted group that joined, trained, travelled and arrived at their intended destination together. Many wanted to perform more exciting duties than they were actually allotted. Norma Best would have preferred a job driving overseas, somewhere on the front line, but this was not to be. She had to be content with clerical work, remembering being first at Preston then at Sinfin Lane, Derby, where she stayed in 'civvy billets' and had a good time.

Esther Armagon trained in Edinburgh as a wireless operator, ending up at 50 Park Street, near Hyde Park, London. Carol Campbell, whose preference of service would have been the WAAF's or WRNS, but had to settle for the ATS, received her initial training at Pontefract in Yorkshire, spending most of her service life in the North of England attached to Headquarters Section and working for officers in charge of court martials. This she thoroughly enjoyed.

Officer A O Weekes, from Barbados, and Flight Sergeant E A Joseph, from Trinidad & Tobago, members of the RAF Bomber Squadron.

Sergeant L O Lynch, from Jamaica, who served as an air gunner with the RAF from 1942. During his training in Canada he was awarded the air-gunner's trophy for two years running, 1943 & 1944, for obtaining the highest percentage of marks in his course. In his first operational flight over enemy territory he shot down a JU88.

Norma Best, from Belize, joined the RAF as ATS in 1944. She trained at Pallisadoes, Jamaica, and travelled to Britain via the USA, enjoying the luxury of the Queen Mary. After the war she became a teacher, rising to headmistress.

George Haynes, from Barbados, joined the RAF in 1944. Member of Nottingham Westindian Combined Ex-Services Association.

Flying Officer Julian Marryshow, from Grenada, son of Theophilus Albert Marryshow, remembered as Grenada's Father of the Nation. He joined the RAF's 193 Squadron and is seen here in 1944 in a Typhoon.

George Powe, from Jamaica, joined the RAF in 1943 as a wireless operator. He made a sizeable contribution to this book.

Ivor De Souza, from Jamaica. Served in the RAF from 1940 - Flight Lieutenant/Flight Commander to Australian Squadron. He did welfare work at the end of the war.

James McKenzie. Joined the RAF from Jamaica in 1944. Spent many years in Britain before returning home in 1991.

Carol Campbell, from Belize, missed her selection and had to pay her own fare to the USA.

Stanley Hodges, from Jamaica, joined the RAF in 1944. A regular member of the Nottingham Westindian Combined Ex-Services Association until his death in 1993.

Frank Holder, from Guyana. A boxer, athlete and singer of some repute. Voted top male vocalist by *Melody Maker* in 1956.

Ulric Cross, from Trinidad & Tobago, RAF Squadron Leader - DSO/DFC and Bar, reputed to be the highest ranking Westindian in World War II. After flying he performed welfare work at the Colonial Office. After the war he became a high court judge in the Westindies. Later he was appointed High Commissioner for Trinidad & Tobago in the UK.

Carl Brewster, from Barbados, served in the RAF from June 1944. He studied and became a chiropodist after the RAF.

Billy Strachan, left his native Jamaica at the age of 18, travelling to Britain under his own steam, arriving with only £3 in his pocket. Joined the RAF as a wireless operator/air gunner, passing out as a Sergeant. Later he became a pilot officer, flying Wellingtons, Tiger Moths, Stirlings and Lancasters, engaging in raids all over Germany. Qualified as an accountant after the war.

Brewster Athlestone Holder, from Jamaica, joined the RAF in 1944, arriving in Britain in 1945.

Arthur Wint - one of the most outstanding Westindian airmen of World War II. A brilliant athlete who won an Olympic Gold medal for Jamaica at 440 yards in 1948 London games. High-Commissioner for Jamaica in the UK between 1974 and 1978. After the RAF he studied medicine, qualifying as a doctor.

Laurie Phillpotts, from Jamaica. Joined the RAF, arrived in Britain early in 1944, welcomed by the Colonial Secretary Sir Oliver Stanley. Attached to aircrew for different operations as teleprinter/operator.

Pasteur Irons, from Jamaica, among one of the first groundcrew to arrive in Britain via the USA. Among those welcomed by Colonial Secretary, Colonel Sir Oliver Stanley at Liverpool before going on to Filey in Yorkshire.

Esther Armagon, from Jamaica, joined ATC branch of the RAF in 1944. After the war she became a midwife.

Ronald Hall, from Guyana. Joined the RAF in 1940 - passed out as Sergeant. His rise through the ranks became meteoric after it became known he spoke French and Italian fluently.

Alwyn Pindar, from Guyana, joined the RAF in 1944. Member of Ex-Services (UK) Association.

Sid Matthews, from Jamaica, joined the RAF in 1944, serving until 1949.

Eric Hudson, from Jamaica, joined the RAF in 1944, arriving in Britain in 1945. He did his initial training at Melksham, Wiltshire.

Gerald Beard, from
Jamaica, joined the RAF in
1943.

Eric Morrison, from
Jamaica, joined the RAF in
1944. Member of the
Nottingham Westindian
Combined Ex-Services
Association.

Vincent Miller, from
Jamaica, joined the RAF in
1944. A dedicated member
of Nottingham Westindian
Combined Ex-Services
Association. Largely
responsible for the
recording of the 'Jamaica
Interviews'.

THREE GENERATIONS OF MILITARY SERVICE: (Left) Jim Moore, who served in two
World Wars, (centre) his daughter Muriel Reader, who spoke for him in this book and (right)
his grandson

Robert Nathaniel Murray,
from Guyana, served in the
RAF during World War II

The Lord Lieutenant of Nottingham, Sir
Andrew Buchanan, at a VE Day church
service prior to the civic reception for the
Nottingham Westindian Combined Ex-
Services Association on 13th May, 1995.

A group of ATS training recruits recently arrived at their training camp in
November, 1943.

(Above) Stirling bomber - highly popular aircraft flown by Westindian aircrew during World War II.

(Right) Avro 'Anson' sinking a German submarine. Many Westindians either trained or flew in these craft.

(Middle right) Hawker Hurricane - typical of that operated by Westindians during World War II.

(Below) The Wellington bomber - extensively used by many Westindian airmen, including Billy Strachan, during World War II.

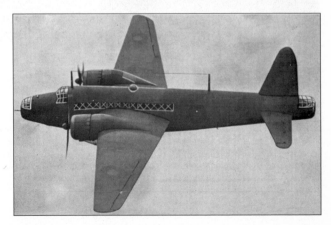

King George VI accompanied by the Queen Mother and princesses Elizabeth and Margaret, inspecting a detachment of Westindian RAF servicemen in Hyde Park, June 1945.

The then Secretary of State for Colonies, the Right Hon. Colonel Oliver Stanley, MC, MP, Air Marshal Sir Arthur Barnet KCB and other high ranking officers of the RAF at the march-past of Westindian recruits who arrived in Britain to take up groundcrew duties. The recruits, all volunteers, numbered nearly 2,000 and were housed in what was once a holiday camp in the north of England.

SOCIALIZING ACTIVITIES

One can, indeed, be forgiven for concluding that this chapter is a misnomer and should well have been entitled - "UNSOCIALIZING ACTIVITIES", for the socializing which in the majority of cases meant dancing, often proved to be nothing more than fights, brawls or unpleasantness. As someone once said:

> "Show me a black serviceman who claimed not to have encountered any prejudice in the UK during the War and I'll show you a liar!"

Westindians - as well as most blacks - felt the hard, cold blast of discrimination and, had everything been equal, could well have enjoyed a much fairer share of the social activities that prevailed. Forty-eight-hour passes, leave and all periods away from camp often presented some dilemma for many Westindian service people from several viewpoints but chiefly climatic, prejudice, out-moded ideas and erroneous beliefs. For instance, it used to be a widely held myth that black men were infinitely more richly 'endowed' sexually than men of other races and this belief presaged many pugilistic encounters between black and white men - particularly when white women were present.

Indigenous members of the forces always had their own homes, relatives or even friends to spend off-duty periods with. American GIs never seemed to encounter so many problems in this respect, neither did members of Commonwealth Services but a predominant number of Westindians suffered the disadvantage of lacking a customary, or even temporary place of refuge in off-duty periods.

One remembers the winter of 1946/47, reputed to be one of the worst in living memory, with snow, lying around for months, at times burying cars, billets, most low buildings and creating havoc with frozen and burst pipes. Although the War had ended several months previously, thousands of service people - British as well as overseas were still in camps throughout the UK and, because of lack of water for cooking, cleaning and ablutions, many camps - Army, Naval and RAF - had to be closed down, causing the enforced leave of personnel.

In these circumstances, many Westindians - particularly those groundcrew members not long in the country - found themselves adrift in extremely adverse wintry conditions, seeking the comfort of clubs, hostels, YMCAs - even lodging houses! There was a handful of Westindians who had found the hands of welcome among understanding indigenous folks, and a minuscule number who were married, James Moore being one of them.

For James Moore, whose war duties took him into France, leave presented a chance to reacquaint himself with his wife and family. His daughter recalls a typical home-coming:

> "He was missing for a little while; mother hadn't heard from him...We were playing on the street early one morning and, when we looked, dad came walking down the street with his blue uniform, red tie and walking stick and that was a great moment. Then you knew daddy was home. Of course when he came home on leave he would always go to the school and ask the teacher if he could take us away that afternoon. He would take us out somewhere, to a movie or something, as a treat."

Those based in Britain, since they were not at the forefront of the War in many respects, would experience off-duty phases while on the camp, as well as periods of leave away from base. On camp itself the groundcrew servicemen, according to Stanley Hodges' recollections, had a mundane existence when not carrying out their operational duties.

> "As far as I'm concerned, there isn't much social life in the services. Being in the company of other men for two to three months at a time, having sing-songs in the NAAFI, drinking cups of tea and not being able to fraternize and socialize freely with the opposite sex isn't what you would call swinging."

On the other hand, off-camp leave was a completely different story for the Westindian servicemen. These off-camp experiences were littered with contradictions, hypocrisy, cultural and class misunderstandings, prejudice and hostility. The hypocrisy existed in that, on one hand the servicemen were befriended by the civilian population, but on the other hand this sign of goodwill was sometimes a facade to conceal other irrationalities and insensitivities. One serviceman vouches for this hypocrisy in the following incident:

> "One day I was walking in Camden Town, North London, with the woman who subsequently became my wife - who was white - when two men passed by. One of them looked at us and remarked: 'Look at them! It oughten to be allowed". Such dehumanizing utterances occurred quite frequently and had the effect of reducing one to less than a man! It was difficult to comprehend how people renowned for their sensitivity could be so overt in their disregard for others."

In addition to these experiences the prejudices emanating from the civilian population, not to mention the taunts and innuendos from fellow servicemen, produced an unsettling effect on the Westindians. To add insult to injury, some servicemen claimed to have been given a lecture on how to conduct themselves in the presence of the local civilian population. George Powe relates:

> "I remember being told that if we were invited to an English home and offered a cup of tea we should refuse first. If offered food, we should pretend not to want it. If we should consume all the food, we were assured that they would not invite us to their homes again, so we must be very discreet and pretend that we were not hungry, even if we were. As regards to the women, they said that we should be careful to avoid sexual intercourse at all cost. If we happened to be 'caught up' with any of the women, we must use our protective gear which was issued to all service-men. We were told about venereal disease because, and in those days there was no penicillin. So if you picked up anything, you would have the nine needles injection. If you picked up any venereal disease at all, you were out of action for at least three months. We were also told that, although the English were a very sensitive sort of people and could be friendly, if they became hostile you might as well pack your bags and go, that's what we were told."

He interpreted the content of this lecture as implying that:

> "...we shouldn't try and offend them. We should be very friendly, we should move around and be, if you like, ambassadors for our country, that was the implication."

In spite of the frequent skirmishes that occurred, many pleasant moments and lasting friendships were often made. An ex-airman recalls that the civilians, mainly women and some elderly men, would come to the camp where he was stationed and would invite the servicemen to tea parties and all sorts of places. He continues:

> "..... we would go round with them and visit their homes but, because of the lecture, many of us, in spite of being hungry, sometimes didn't eat. You see, we sat there and pretended as if we were filled to the brim. We didn't have any food."

On one occasion even the prescribed way to behave given in the lecture had not equipped the Westindian airmen for the idiosyncratic nature of English culture. In another experience of going for tea at a civilian house the same airman came up against Britain's class division:

> "..... we went to a woman's place I went with my mate and because we made complimentary remarks about her maid she told us not to come back. She...objected to us making such remarks because .... 'that young woman was just a maid' and to go to her house and make such remarks about her maid, well, they must be kept in their place. She said the only reason why she associated with us was because we were Jamaican service-men fighting for King and country, otherwise she would not associate with us. She didn't invite us out of friendship. In other words she was trying to make the troops comfortable so that they could be very efficient fighting machines."

Being invited to a tea party at a civilian house, and the reception the Westindian servicemen received from women, was in stark contrast to what the recruits were originally told as they journeyed to Britain:

> "...when we went out the first night, the NCO's words that no white women would consort with us proved all wrong. We found most of them to be most friendly and sociable. Many of the chaps made lasting friendships. Another thing I noticed was that they had a very convenient password in those days, 'would you like a cup of tea?' This carried a lot of meaning, more than met the eyes."

The association between British women and black service-men at times was greatly motivated by curiosity. The racial ideas that existed about black men seemed to have slipped into the consciousness of the public and were accepted as reality by some individuals. In one instance while dancing George Powe recalls:

> ".... some of the girls would quite discreetly move their hands near your rectum to find out whether you had a tail. That was the kind of experience that we had sometimes."

Stanley Hodges also instances:

> "A mate and I were trying to date two teenage girls at a skating rink in Manchester. I said to this girl, 'What about it?' She replied 'No thanks, I want to be thrilled not tortured'. I must admit I was a bit taken aback. Eventually I think I got her gist, if you know what I mean."

Robert Murray suggests that some of the responses that the servicemen elicited were partly due to where they were situated at the time:

> "People weren't so much prejudiced as insular and shy and had to be brought out of themselves. It must be remembered that Melksham, where we found ourselves, was not a city - only a very small, prim market town - where everything was peaceful and sedate. All of this was suddenly broken by all these Westindians. I mean - three thousand - all very 'rusty' and all looking for fun and companionship and all that kind of thing. Perhaps a few wanted to take the plunge and entertain the boys but dared not for fear of the 'prying eyes' and wagging tongues."

Stanley Hodges confesses that:

> "Apart from the frivolous side, we met ordinary English families who treated us not as studs or lovers but as ordinary humans."

He goes on to mention two white families who would accommodate them, in their homes whenever they visited Bolton, and he considers these people to be "brave, kind and caring," - especially in the hostile climate that existed towards black people at the time. In a similar vein Adrian Neysnich describes the people in the region where he was stationed around Preston as being "friendly", "loving", and "wonderful", with the area itself being clean. He sums up these people in these terms:

"I wish the world was like these people in this little vicinity."

However, these individuals seemed to be few and far between. Quite often when walking around the streets during off-duty, the Westindian airmen would be stared at and had racist comments directed at them. Stanley Hodges recollects some of the ideas that existed and were circulated about black people:

"Rumours were being spread that we came from jungles, lived in trees, had tails and so on. But when they discovered for themselves that this wasn't so, and that we were friendly, intelligent, fit and good dancers, their attitudes changed, especially the women!"

Robert Murray claims that in some cases it wasn't clear whether people's behaviour was based on racist ideas, resulting in discrimination or prejudice, or would be more suitably understood in terms "of utter fear and sheer ignorance!". He recalls one episode that exemplifies his sentiments on this:

"I was stationed at an operational training unit in Buckinghamshire. There was a nearby farmhouse which sold beautiful early morning breakfasts - teas, coffee, bacon, eggs, etc. This made a change from the camps which always dished up watery scrambled eggs - horrible stuff! One day there was a new young girl assistant who looked apprehensive as soon as she saw me. I could see her getting whiter and whiter and as I asked for what I wanted she started to shake - trembling like a leaf. I always took a sort of sadistic pleasure in exploiting such situations. So, as she was laying the breakfast, I bared my teeth and snapped at her. The girl dropped everything, shrieked and ran out of the building, down a lane and literally vanished! I just killed myself laughing, but such was the educational system that existed in those days that the young girl's head was filled with the nonsense about black people being savages. So terrified was she that, of the open window and door that stood next to each other in front of her, she opted to leap through the window. The landlord came in and said he wasn't surprised; she hadn't been anywhere - hadn't seen life. He'd been around the world."

Pasteur Irons recalls that when he and others first visited Blackpool, people would run from them, shouting: "The blacks are coming." On another occasion also in Blackpool, the landlady asked the names of the boys, and when Pasteur said his name was Irons, she immediately retorted. "Oh, no. We supply all the irons here. We don't need yours!"

> "Of course kids would say, 'Look at that blackie', or 'There is a blackie coming'."

The prevalence of these ideas and their acceptance as fact were exemplified by an incident between a black serviceman and a child. This incident also reveals that ignorance of others different to oneself that formed the basis of some of the problems that existed between the black and white individuals. Adrian Neysnich recalls:

> "It sounds funny but I went to Preston from where we always got our food, and one little boy ran up and said, 'we were told that you have tails, show us your tail!' Well, I said, 'Come here, who told you that black people have tails?' He said, 'My mummy told me that.' I said, 'When you go back tell your mum that there is no such thing as a tail on a black man, not at all, no tail on anybody at all. We are just people like you but because of the sunshine, and over the generations, we became dark.' The next time we went there, the mother came out and spoke to us, asking who gave her son that information, and you know, we were invited to tea and became regular visitors to those people in Preston."

At times the naivety of the black servicemen tended to leave them vulnerable as opportunists sometimes sought to take advantage of them. One experience that Robert Murray refers to exposes such an occasion, even though he was with a friend who had been in Britain for some years and who acted as a chaperon:

> "This occurred on my very first leave which was in Cardiff. I was accompanied by a Jamaican friend - Peters - who'd visited the city before. He'd been in the UK longer than I. We were staying in a hostel. Peters and I had got up, washed and dressed and were debating what we would have for breakfast when there was a knock at the door. A respectable-looking man was standing there. He asked what we would like for breakfast. We said that we were just about to go down to the breakfast-room to get it. He assured us that it was part of the normal service for him to bring our breakfast to us. We gave him 10 shillings each - two 10-bob notes. We never saw him again. On making enquiries downstairs, we were told that there was no such service. This incident, of course, had nothing to do with racism, prejudice or the colour bar. It

was just an out and out 'con' but it was a revelation to us."

When confrontation did occur the civilian population's inclination was to believe the account of the white individual involved in the incident. Gerald Beard recalls facing this mentality in a rather peculiar kind of encounter with a member of the civilian population, which typified this general tendency:

> "I think I was taking a girl home, like, and after I'd taken her part way she directed me to where to catch my train. But being unaccustomed to the place I got lost. I eventually would have found my way but it would have taken me a long time. Then I saw an Englishman, so I asked him. Well, I was, green to what people were up to. But I remember he took me to a dead end road, then he started grabbing at my trousers; I was frightened .... I began to shout! .... I knew a woman who lived across the road. She opened down her window and shouted, 'Leave him alone', leave him alone! ..... I said, 'This man started to pull at my trousers.' The culprit had already taken to his heels."

Leave offered an opportunity for the Westindian servicemen to find out what their compatriots were doing. Subsequently the servicemen had "a pretty good idea" of other servicemen's activities in Britain for:

> "Wherever we were stationed we visited London regularly, either on leave or on 48-hour passes. Most of us used to meet at a hostel, which I believe was called "The 77 Club", so-called because it was situated at 77 Wimpole Street, London, where we chatted and exchanged the latest information concerning one another....So most of us kept in touch with what others were doing by these visits to the hostel and obtained news about those who didn't frequent London but visited other cities instead. Another meeting point in London ·we favoured was the Paramount dance-hall."

These occasions were even more important for aircrew individuals than for groundcrew servicemen. As previously mentioned, Ulric Cross states the only time that he met other black servicemen was essentially when he went to London on leave. Ivor De'Souza, another aircrewman, claims that some special social events were organised and funded by the Colonial Office, for instance when he met Sir Gary Sobers, a famous Caribbean cricketer. For Stanley Hodges the aim was abundantly clear:

> "When on leave the main object was to meet and have fun with the opposite sex."

Nevertheless, the main pre-occupation during the Westindian serviceman's off-duty periods took entirely different channels because of the need to defend themselves:

> "Even though we were fighting a practical war, as far as we, the Westindians were concerned, it seemed as if we had to fight a war on our own for survival. How that situation came about was very difficult for any of us to explain but it was there and during that period there were many, many unpleasant incidents."

This statement, by Stanley Hodges, encapsulates the predominant recollections of most Caribbean airmen's off-duty experiences. He goes to state that:

> "During that period, as far as we were concerned, the motto was 'kill or be killed', and we didn't mean the enemy ..... I have never laid a hand on a German or Italian soldier, who was supposed to be the enemy, but I had to fight or run like hell to save my skin when confronted by the so-called allies."

The extent of the antagonism which prevailed during periods of leave between the Westindian airmen and other groups of service-men as well as with the civilian population is revealed in George Powe's comments:

> ".... you may not believe it but I used to fight at least twice a week for the first two or three years that I was in Britain."

The harmony that existed between the allies, that is, the Americans and British, contrasted sharply with that which prevailed between the Westindian servicemen and the white Americans and, to a certain extent, the British. This antagonism, according to Robert Murray, was a result of the "unwanted fraternization" between black servicemen and white women. In James Mckenzie's estimation, black service-men's:

105

" .... meeting and mixing with girls caused a lot of friction as the English men did not like us blacks meeting their girls."

The attitude that existed at the time is reflected in George Powe's perception of how white men viewed such interactions:

" .... if you spoke to a woman, you find that the woman was 'being insulted and that would start a fight."

A comment recalled by Gerald Beard further supports the ethos that existed. He recalls being told:

"I am not going to have you niggers coming here and fooling about with our women."

These attitudes ran counter to the experiences that most Westindian servicemen encountered when they arrived in Britain. On arrival in Britain, women, especially those in the forces, were actively encouraged to befriend the black service-men. Now they were dissuaded from such socializing. Women who were seen to persist with such associations faced scorn, contempt and scathing abuse. Robert Murray reflects:

"The Westindians were disliked for one major reason - always women, always girls, always the white men not wanting their women to fraternize with those blacks. It was this singular thing that caused fights in the past and that was why one was brewing now. One or two of the WAAFs on the camp were kindly disposed towards some of the lads and, of course, the men didn't like it. The white airmen used to start off by telling the girls that they were no good and generally deriding them in all manner of ways. Of course the WAAFs would come back and tell the lads what was being said to them and they would scream, 'This means War!'.

One incident recalled by Stanley Hodges details the all too familiar pretext, skirmish and conclusion of such a violent confrontation. while at a dance:

"Scottish soldiers came up to us and one remarked 'Hi, darkie! I see you are dancing with white girls! If you were in Germany you would have been shot, you black bastards!' This sort of statement took us by surprise and we were stunned!"

This remark sparked off a fight and Stanley Hodges suspected that the whole incident was planned. He goes on to expand:

"There were about four soldiers involved who made the first confrontation, but during the scuffle we realised that another four or five civilian men had joined them.... We were surrounded and attacked by a group of these same people. In the meantime the four of us now, were heavily involved in the scuffle. I briefly observed at one stage that one of my mates was lying on the floor unconscious being kicked and thumped. At this stage I saw a chair being waved and aimed at me and somehow I managed to absorb the impact and eventually avoided the main force of the fighting. However it ended in a very short and abrupt manner, because one of the civilian attackers was stabbed in the stomach and that seemed to bring the whole thing to an abrupt end."

The police were called and Stanley Hodges was wrongly accused of the stabbing by the locals. He continues his account of the incident by stating:

"I was arrested that night and taken to the local police station in Bolton and charged for malicious wounding or something to that effect. My other two mates were not charged but they followed it up. The authorities on my camp were notified and officers were sent from the camp to represent me in court a couple of days later."

The outcome of this affair saw Stanley Hodges being acquitted of all the charges due to insufficient evidence. Again this incident was illustrative of the tendency to point an accusing finger at any black service-man within the vicinity of an incident in which a white person was involved. This would often lead to legal wrangling and the involvement of the Colonial Office, who would usually send someone to represent the defendant, as Ulric Cross's previous account details.

Gerald Beard was another Westindian who was wrongly accused of a crime. He recollects:

".... on my way to Piccadilly, Manchester, a lot of other chaps kept running towards me. Then I found myself at the spot where it was supposed to happen. A big crowd was there. In the crowd a policeman was there, I spoke to the policeman for about twenty minutes when I heard the people say, 'that's him! That's him.' The policeman came over to me and asked, 'Is it you?' I didn't know what he meant, so he said, 'Well, these folks say it's you who just killed this man,' and when I turned around and looked I saw blood. He said they just took his body away to the Ancourt Hospital. So when the policeman realised he had no coloured man to hold, he turned around and said to me, 'It's a fair country. You will get justice.' Just like that, and then they took me to Strangeways prison that night in Manchester. I think I was there for about seven or eight weeks until Manley come from Jamaica to defend me."

This court case attracted individuals from all parts of the country but was not destined to last any great length of time. Norman Manley senior, an eminent barrister and who later became the Prime Minister of Jamaica, represented Gerald Beard. At the commencement of the court proceedings, Manley immediately questioned the wisdom of initiating charges against Gerald Beard and set about discrediting the policeman and the individual who claimed he saw Gerald Beard commit the act. Gerald Beard describes the proceedings of this case in some detail:

"Well, even the very man who said he saw me cracked when Manley put him on the spot under cross-examination. When asked how far he was from the scene of the stabbing he replied: 'Pretty near enough.'

'How near is pretty near?' asked Manley.

'Well, I was at London Road Station, about 50 yards around the corner,'

Manley erupted! 'So you are telling this court that you clearly saw this man stabbing another man from 50 yards around a corner from London Road Station to Piccadilly, about 50 yards away at night?'

The witness wouldn't answer, he knew it was impossible. Manley suggested the witness could not do it during the day never mind at night?'

'What position was this man standing in?' asked Manley. The witness could not remember.

'Do you remember what hand the defendant used in the stabbing?'

'His right, sir,' the man said.

'May I inform you the defendant is left-handed, and therefore could not have stabbed the man in that place from the position in which he was standing?'"

Norman Manley proceeded to rip the prosecution apart, discrediting the witnesses, proving that the defendant, Gerald Beard, being left-handed, could not have committed the offence for which he was charged. He (Norman Mandley) did not care for the very off-handish manner in which the prosecution approached the case and was particularly severe on the Police Inspector both for this fact and for not using the correct form of address in replying to his questions as a King's Counsel. The Judge, Lord Chief Justice Goddard, voiced his approval:

"Yes, address him correctly." Then, still addressing the Inspector, he said, "According to my recollection, this is the second time you've brought such a case before me." The Police Inspector was later understood to have been stripped of his rank and two witnesses dealt with for perjury. Needless to say, Gerald Beard was acquitted to the satisfaction and delight of his compatriots and supporters.

Identity has always presented a problem, for it often used to be said in those far off days during and immediately after the last War, when the number of blacks in the UK was limited to those in the services plus a few residing in the docks areas, that it was difficult to tell one from the other; and this inability to recognise and identify Westindians nearly always proved to be their saving grace in cases of the type just mentioned.

Ronald Hall, whose rise through the ranks became meteoric when his facility with languages revealed itself, found himself in the Colonial Office when his tours of operations ended and being asked to represent Westindians in Court Martials. He recollects his first case:

> "The NCOs indulged in the habit of entering the billets at getting up time in the mornings to rouse the fellows. They would switch the lights on ordering: 'Wakey, wakey! Rise and shine! etc."

Sometimes these peremptory orders were accompanied by the banging of chairs and tables and the kicking of beds. The Westindians on this particular occasion, took exception to this behaviour feeling that such treatment was only levelled towards them. They therefore decided to do something about it. This took the form of removing all the light-bulbs one night and, on the following morning at reveille, attacked all those who entered bellowing orders in the dark, it being winter. Of course, the authorities would not tolerate this kind of behaviour and instituted Court Martial proceedings. Ronald Hall, now a Flight- Lieutenant, remained silent throughout the hearing, listening to all the accusations and counter-accusations with one consideration on his mind, which was: if they had difficulty in identifying the lads in normal light, how did they manage in the dark? So when asked for his comments, he ordered the Sergeant who claimed to have identified the Westindians to stand outside for a minute, then he got the Westindians, A.C. Johnson, A.C. Williams and A.C. Henderson, to stand together. When the Sergeant re-entered, he failed to identify the three airmen correctly, getting them completely mixed up. The case was dismissed.

The media also joined the chorus of voices objecting to black service-men associating with White women. Most Westindian servicemen will recall a place called "Paramount Dance-Hall" which was often frequented by them during their off-duty periods. This place was located on Tottenham Court Road, London, and was a very short distance from where the servicemen's hostel stood on Wimpole Street. An ex-serviceman reflects:

> ".... the Paramount was the only dance-hall where you would find a substantial number of Westindians. It was the focal point for the meeting our comrades - both those you saw regularly and those you hadn't seen for some time and, of course, seeing the girls who came in abundance to socialize."

He goes on to assert that the woman there were:

> "Almost entirely English, of course, but with a fair sprinkling of Irish, Welsh, Scots and Continentals. It must be remembered that in those days there were very few black girls around. Only a mere handful was in the Armed Forces and they were widely dispersed throughout the country."

Because of the predominance of white women attending this dance hall, Robert Murray remembers the Paramount "creating some ill-feeling in the outside world":

"Many felt that the sort of intimate socializing that went on there should not have been allowed. The newspapers had a field day, talking about 'ill-timed and unwanted fraternising,' and that blacks and whites should never be allowed to mix in such a way. I remember reading an article entitled 'Don't let this go on.' They described the Paramount as a hive for this and that and a veritable den of iniquity. As usual they accused those that frequented the place as pedlars of dope and dealers in guns and hinted covertly that the girls were nothing less than tarts. They suggested that the place should be bombed."

However, these comments about the people who attended the Paramount for entertainment were merely media hype, trivialization and misrepresentation, as he continues to comment:

"I can only say that during the time I went there, I saw none of these things. It was all a concerted attempt to besmirch the name of the Paramount who dared to permit black servicemen to pass through its doors. I could never put my hand on my heart and say categorically that nothing untoward ever happened there this would be folly. But the newspapers, for their own ends, blew things up out of all proportion. The vast majority of the boys and girls were of impeccable character and went there simply to enjoy themselves. Many made relationships that have lasted to the present day."

Dance halls, like the Paramount, were essentially places that provided the Westindian servicemen with a hospitable environment in which they could relax and feel accepted, especially by the women who attended this place as the statement by Robert Murray declares:

"Women who befriended the Westindian servicemen were a much-maligned body of people, being objects of derision, jibes and taunts. Yet most never wavered in their allegiance and loyalty when the going was toughest and no amount of praise could be too high for them. In the very early days they remained a tower of strength and were among the few to extend the hand of welcome to the lads."

He goes on to summarize the character of the Paramount in the following manner:

"It was a place where loves were made and loves were lost. Among the enjoyment and pleasure, it was a place of brief relationships and long relationships, of rivalries, of passions and intense jealousies. Above all

111

it was a place that could never be forgotten. It belonged to that era and that era alone."

These detailed and numerous accounts of "bust-ups, scuffles, and fights" that occurred between black and white servicemen, were engraved on the recollections of the war experience for Westindian airmen. These melees would occur mostly against the Americans "because of racial jealousy," and rarely with the British servicemen. As George Powe states:

> "Yes there were one or two fights, but we found that most of the fights were with the Americans. The Americans would call us niggers, and ask questions like 'where are your tails!' and all those kind of things."

As a result of this type of hostility, the typical reaction to the situation by black servicemen was to arm themselves and only venture out in groups. This response is revealed in the comments made by Stanley Hodges, George Powe and Robert Murray. Stanley Hodges comments:

> "Whenever we went on leave, we always went together in threes or fours, never alone, and would always carry formidable means of self defence."

Robert Murray concurs with this defensive posture when he affirms:

> ".... at that camp I had a knife. I had bought it because there were incidents in certain towns where the boys were beaten up, stabbed and that sort of thing. I therefore decided that if I was ever attacked by gangs, whether civilians or servicemen, I was not going to take it lying down. Somebody was going to get it. I would retaliate but I always hoped that I would never have to use it."

George Powe remembers one incident in which a fellow Westindian serviceman ventured out alone and what happened to him and the subsequent action taken by the Westindian service-men:

> ".... one night a chap, called 'Mushett', a young fellow, went into one of the villages, and he was beaten up by the Americans, so we decided that we would go into that village and beat the Americans up. One of the

reasons why we were so upset about this was that we told this chap not to go on his own. A woman rescued him, phoned for the ambulance and he was taken back to the camp half dead. So we went into town, about five hundred of us, armed to the teeth with knuckle-dusters, daggers and the lot. The fight lasted about two hours, and we cleared the Yanks out of the village. We were there about three months and for the next three months no Yanks dared to come in the town."

However, this was not always the response to Westindian fights with American service-men. In most cases the black service-men were seen as a problem. Therefore, in an attempt to resolve this conflict, some individuals attempted to ban black service-men from using certain amenities and from going to certain places. One ex-serviceman recalls hearing a rumour of an attempt to prohibit black service-men from entering Bath and Bristol, near to where he was stationed, because these places were frequently used by the Americans who had influence in the area. Gerald Beard recalls an incident which occurred when a Westindian service-man faced such a ban, which reveals the resentment and frustration felt by the Westindian servicemen to what they perceived as unfair treatment. A confrontation ensued in which the Westindians, as usual, were placed behind bars for the night and released the following day.

Pasteur Irons still harbours memories of being in Blackpool on an MTD Training Course. When going into the town one night, Westindians came under attack by Americans who 'bit off more that they could chew' and ended up very much the worse for wear. To their great surprise, the Westindians found themselves lined up in front of their Commanding Officer the following morning. He told them:

"You can't come here fighting our allies!"

He posted them immediately en block to Bristol to continue their MTD Training.

In those days nine fights out of ten involving Westindians and white Americans owed their origins 'to word or deed' by the White Americans who, because of their policy towards their own blacks in America, just could not countenance any situation in which fraternization was permitted and this objection often went beyond

113

their own sphere of influence. What the Westindians, as British Subjects did, should never have concerned them. Yet, such was the case. Ronald Hall, arriving in Gloucester from fighting the Axis Powers in Italy, newly promoted to the rank of officer, and invited to an R.A.F dance, fell victim to a vicious assault by a white American for no other reason than dancing with a white woman - a dance to which he, as an American, should never have been allowed admittance anyway.

Although Ronald Halls treated the incident with a certain amount of jocularity, the British as well as the American authorities viewed the matter extremely seriously, so much so that at the subsequent Court Martial of the perpetrator of the aggression against an officer of HM Forces, he was given a two year prison sentence coupled with a dishonourable discharge from the American Army. In addition, Ronald Hall received a letter of apology from General Dwight, D. Eisenhower, Commander in Chief of the Allied Armed Forces, who very much regretted the incident.

Gerald Beard and another serviceman both narrate incidents that resulted in a fatality. Gerald Beard recalls;

> "Well many of us there were Jamaicans, Kitisians and so forth, and these white Americans started to pick a fight straight away with these chaps.... trying to be funny once with a coloured Yank, you know. Well, one of them was calling him nigger and thing.....I am not saying it's right, and I am not saying it's wrong, he just held his head and pulled him outside where the white American met his fate!"

While the other service-man reflects on a different incident:

> "There was a restaurant in Soho not far from the Paramount which blacks as well as whites, particularly white Yanks, frequented. One night I walked into the restaurant and a heated row was going on between a Westindian and a white Yank. The Westindian dished out a terrible beating to the Yank who dashed out of the restaurant, returning shortly afterwards with a revolver, stood at the door, gunned the Westindian down without pity or compunction and departed, leaving everyone stunned and shaken. It was understood that the Yank was arrested and charged with murder. One heard nothing more about the case."

Hence deaths on both the Westindian and American side occurred. Robert Murray narrates, in great detail, one violent confrontation between British and Westindian service-men:

"There was trouble brewing at this particular camp. The 30 or 40 Westindians were not liked by the white RAF men.... So this confrontation seemed inevitable. It was approaching Christmas and on most camps there was always a Christmas dance in the NAAFI (Navy, Army and Air Force Institute). All fights seemed to originate in the NAAFI because this was where everyone met to smoke, drink and to socialize generally. Nothing galvanises people into fights more than drink.

On the Christmas-Eve night the dance was being held in the NAAFI and, of course, the white airmen were spoiling for a fight. Their attitude was that no Westindian was going to attend the dance with any WAAF. However, the unfavourable comments made to the WAAFs by the white Airmen, coupled with the very strained atmosphere, tended to put them off. Many had decided not to attend the dance for fear of trouble. So the Westindians weren't going with them but instead invited girls from the nearby towns who were great fans of theirs. They must have bussed in over one hundred girls - all looking gorgeous compared to the WAAFs dressed in their dark blue uniforms which looked dull and mundane. On the other hand, the civilian girls in their different coloured dresses and wearing lipstick and make-up caused the white airmen to be bitterly jealous, even though they had their own WAAFs. The air was charged with envy, the atmosphere being extremely tense!

The white airmen were determined to have a show-down and made their intentions clear from the very outset. As they were dancing, they would draw quite near and elbow and trip-up the Westindians. Of course, a terrible fight erupted. The boys, heavily outnumbered, came in for somewhat of a mauling. The NAAFI was completely smashed, it looked like a battlefield in no time."

He continues:

"I never went to these events - in fact, I couldn't dance in those days, although I was to learn sometime later, in any case I was always studying for something or another, being what you would call a real book-worm. So I was the only one left in the billet though not in my own room which was at the end, as all the boys had gone to the dance, apart from those who'd gone into the nearest town. All of a sudden the door to the billet burst open and three lads rushed towards me shouting agitatedly 'Sarge! Sarge! Give me your knife!' I, taken back, hardly had time to ask what for? They were so worked up they ignored me. They dashed to my room which, fortunately, was locked, the key safely in my pocket, so they couldn't get at my knife. Feeling that they would get nowhere with me, and that time was passing by, they dashed out again, leaving me still clueless as to what had happened. I had no time to stop them. I remained in the billet.

However, although in ignorance as to the origins of their anger, one didn't have to be a genius to hazard a guess. I did not take too kindly to their unsolicited attempts to enter my room, so I was not altogether displeased at their lack of success in procuring the knife. Nevertheless, I suddenly became possessed with nervousness, knowing what might happen to the lads in such a highly excitable and volatile state.

In the meantime, some of the lads had begun to filter back into the billet from the dance looking much the worse for wear and not being in any mood to relate exactly what had occurred at the dance. Judging by the state they were in, words were unnecessary."

He continues:

"Shortly afterwards, minding my own business, being deeply preoccupied   with 'The Origin's of the English Language,' there was another peremptory interruption when the Commanding Officer with his retinue of officers and NCOs charged into the billet. His entire attitude was belligerent and accusatorial as he accosted:

'Where is Sergeant Murray!! Where is Sergeant Murray!!' 'I approached him.' 'Sergeant Murray! I'm dumbfounded! Never seen such savagery in all my 25 years in the RAF!' He was telling me this as if I had anything to do with it. 'One of my airmen has been brutally stabbed on my camp, my camp! This is an outrage! The airman in question had been out with his girl-friend and was returning to the base when one of your boys pounced on him and stabbed him. This is outrageous!'

He had lost all sense of decorum and was acting like a man demented. 'You have brought shame and disgrace on my camp. All you Westindians are confined to camp. I -'

'Excuse me, Sir,' I ventured to intervene, trying to get a word in edge-ways.

'Are you certain it was done by Westindians?'

'Course, we're certain - no one else would commit such a dastardly act!'

'Then you've got tangible proof, Sir?' I asked

'Well, I-I,' he stalled as rationality began to return.

'As good as', one of his officers chipped in.

'That's not good enough,' I said, 'either you saw or you didn't. If you have got any proof I'd like you to name the airman and I'll do the rest.' They all stood rigid, not knowing what to say or do."

While the Commanding Officer was "ranting and raving," the rest of the Westindian servicemen were equally being vociferous in their opinions:

"... all of the boys were screaming and shouting abuse at him, treating him as if he were nothing, shouting: 'Who gwine confine us?'...and...'What for?' and 'shut up! .... get out of here.'"

This behaviour was untypical as instanced in the comment by the narrator who states:

"In normal circumstances such behaviour in the presence of the Commanding Officer - let alone directed at him - would have been a chargeable offence. But he had lost this right by his aggressive and partisan approach as neither he nor his entourage of officers and NCOs could understand what the boys were saying in their patois and highly-agitated state. In the end, he stormed off saying 'We're not going to stand here listening to mumbo jumbo and paraphernalia!"

Although there was no evidence to link any Westindian airmen to the incident involving the white service-man, the Westindian service-men felt they would have been vulnerable to whatever action the RAF authorities saw as appropriate if the Colonial Office did not exist. This fact was recognised in the following observation by one ex-airman when he insisted:

"... the Colonial Office was the stabilising factor - our protectors, with many Westindian officers there. Had there been no Colonial Office the Commanding Officer probably could have done what he liked. But always there was the Colonial Office - and questions would be asked in Parliament and this sort of thing."

The Colonial Office was informed and a representative of theirs did make some extensive enquiries but, in the end, nothing came of this. Despite intense speculation no-one was found guilty, in fact there was not even a trial. The repercussions of this incident were that all Westindian service-men were posted to an isolated camp, a place called "Strubby," near Alford Town in Lincolnshire. Strubby was described as once being:

> ".... an operational station where Lancaster and Halifax Bombers used to land and take off regularly but now it was completely deserted. Only the runway remained. There was a Flying-Officer in command and I, being a Sergeant, was second in command. Discipline was non-existent in the absence of the RAF police or a guard room. In fact, it was not unusual for the CO, to confine a man to camp for some mis-demeanour or other, and then be seen drinking with the same confined man in the pub that very night. It was then I realised that doing nothing was harder than the most strenuous work. It was plain boring. With Mablethorpe only 6 miles away, and Skegness only 12 miles, each of us was issued with a bicycle. All we had to do was to cycle off to the seaside every day. One sizeable RAF lorry was put at our disposal which one of our boys was in charge of. Any time we wanted to go anywhere he would drive us. We used to go to Mablethorpe every evening in time for the opening of the pubs at about 6.00pm. Then at 8 o'clock we would make our way to the dance just across the road. It was at these dances in Mablethorpe that I - with the drink in me - learned to dance and there were many willing to teach me."

It has often been said and it is, perhaps, a truism that the greatest cause of fear is fear itself - a dictum very apparent in those far-off days of the War when Westindians combed dance-halls, circumvented dance-floors, seeking partners only to be confronted by negative head-shakes and hasty, undignified retreats. Not that the Westindians suffered from dislike or dancing ineptitudes, for most of them were perceived to be capable movers when forced to dance among themselves but the faces of the on-looking women conveyed uncertainty and fear of the unknown - more pertinently, fear of others; for there were prying eyes and wagging tongues. No-one wanted to step out of line. No-one wanted to be seen breaking ranks and appearing to be deviating from what was considered to be 'prim and proper'; and yet, as always on such occasions, the refusals were never completely unanimous amongst all the women present.

There were always a few itching to 'have a go' jiving, boogie-woogying and beebopping with the Westindians, and one acquiescence usually signalled another and another - until a trickle became a torrent. The boys, therefore, were never totally bereft of partners. Hence this chapter cannot be closed without dispelling the impression that life for the Westindian in the forces in general - and in the RAF in particular - consisted of nothing else but unpleasantness.

Neither were their off-duty activities limited to London. While many proceeded to London in their free periods, a majority hardly ever visited the capital but sought enjoyment in the other large conurbations such as Birmingham, Manchester, Leeds, Bristol, Sheffield, Newcastle, Sunderland, Derby, Nottingham, Leceister. Some even permeated in smaller places like Bath, Long Eaton, Burton-on-Trent, Stafford and Stoke-on-Trent. Whilst some found the Paramount in London welcoming, others preferred quieter venues - Nottingham, Bath or Derby or the cosiness of the Royal Dance Hall in Long Eaton or the Skating Rink in Manchester; or, perhaps, haunts just outside Manchester, in places like Heywood, Oldham, Rochdale or Bolton.

Three weeks after Billy Strachan completed his initial training as a wireless operator/air-gunner in Blackpool, he met Joyce in a rather circuitous manner. She was working in the Ministry of Health which had been dispersed from London to a grand Blackpool hotel. He recalls:

> "I'd gone to the ballroom in the Winter Gardens where I'd met a rather attractive girl, and we had arranged to meet the next night; but when I arrived at her house, she'd stood me up.' Then her flatmate, Joyce, came downstairs - and, that was that. It was a typical wartime courtship. We wrote to each other regularly - Joyce, everyday, and I, once a week. We snatched moments together whenever training allowed."

Westindian service-men even wandered further afield, sampling Cardiff, Glasgow, Belfast, Dublin. One chap, who lacked the art of dancing when he joined up, soon learned, reportedly with the aid of the bottle and thereafter set out to do much better than ambling around the dance floor. In 1946, he recalls dancing every day (and night) excluding Good Friday and Christmas. Stationed at Stafford, he frequented Stoke-on-Trent and remembers afternoon dances at Trenthan Gardens as well as regularly patronizing venues in Birmingham.

On being posted near to London, he continued his dancing

exploits by visiting the Paramount every afternoon (Sundays included) from 3pm to 6pm, then returning for the evening sessions from 7pm to 11pm. On Fridays, after the last waltz at 11pm, he made for the nearest underground ablutions, freshened up, and felt rejuvenated to face the session commencing at the Lyceum Ballroom in the Strand at midnight and finishing at 4.00 in the morning when he and others would saunter across to the nearby LYONS CORNER HOUSE to replenish with tea, sausage-rolls and sandwiches until the buses and tube trains started to run at 6 am when either the 77 Club in Wimpole Street or camp would beckon.

On leave, his first task after procuring a hostel accommodation was to ascertain the location of the nearest dance-hall. He remembers being ejected from The Hammersmith Palais in West London with his partner for jiving on a night not ear-marked for that purpose and compares this ignominy with his indulgence in the same activity in Green's Playhouse, Glasgow, where a specially roped-off area catered for his form of dancing - a more sensible arrangement. He developed ball-room dancing as well. In this way, he became highly proficient in the art of dancing, being targeted by the lasses - particularly in 'Excuse-me' pieces.

The above-mentioned story should not be taken in isolation as it bore typicality for many Westindian service people at the time who used much of their free periods in exactly the same manner - utilizing their leave to indulge in favourite pastimes.

Mention has previously been made to MacDonald-Bailey and Arthur Wint in athletics, Nadia Catouse, Cy Grant and Frank Holder in entertainment but there were dozens of others who either gave birth to, or developed, their talents in different fields while still in the RAF - talents at football, weight-lifting, boxing, billiards and snooker.

Frank Holder - although a budding vocalist - maintained his fitness by partaking in athletics and boxing. In athletics, stationed at RAF Cranwell in Lincolnshire with MacDonald-Bailey, the Olympic Sprinter, both often trained together - Holder once achieving 9.9 seconds in the 100 yards sprint; and in boxing, he represented RAF Hullavington and RAF Cosford. In the field of entertainment, many remember him singing at the Paramount, Hammersmith Palais and the Lyceum Ballroom while still in his RAF uniform to the strains of Ivor Kirchin, Joe Loss and other bands.

Others who progressed in boxing were the Jamaican, Rennie Davis, who became the Middle Weight Champion of the RAF, Jackson Bill, Johnny Carrington and Percy Lewis - a Trinidadian, who later turned professional, doing quite well for a time. In those early days, of course, blacks were not allowed to fight for Commonwealth or Empire titles until Cliff Anderson, a Guyanese, became the very first to do so when he tackled Al Philips - a Scotsman - only to be declared the loser contrary to the opinion of most of those present. This injudicious decision, however, failed to deter the ever-increasing flow of black people into the profession until today when no such restriction exists.

But it was cricket - that delightful summer game - which presented the greatest opportunity for socializing in the RAF for it embodied a way of life both for Westindians and English alike, proffering a common language that all participants understood; a concerted appeal might mean - a walk; a brilliant stroke could herald a four or a six! There were no arguments, no threats, no fights - just on with the game!

Of all the recollections about the socializing aspect of military life, the servicemen expressed vibrant memories of cricket matches played during the War between a Westindian eleven from RAF Stafford and a team of burly policemen from Burslem, Stoke-on-Trent - all six footers who skittled the Westindians out for a mere twenty-three runs much to their displeasure and chagrin. Such humiliation in the presence of an enthusiastic local crowd stirred the boys from the Caribbean into action causing them to redress the balance by removing the 'Coppers' for just eighteen runs. Honours were then regarded as even. But in the aftermath the mechanics of the game became irrelevant - forgotten as the tea, biscuits and sandwiches took over and the beer flowed like water. Then these provincial 'Coppers' set about revealing the extent of their knowledge of Westindian cricket when talking about such by-gone men as Leary Constantine, Manny Martindale and George Headley with Westindian retorts of Les Ames, Patsy Hendren, Larwood and Voce. Many games were played in, and ended, in the same spirit as the one in question.

Socializing, of course, takes many forms and the Westindians - both men and women- utilized most forms to the full. Another aspect of socializing is that one need not socialize with others. People could amuse themselves in the company of others without ever consorting with them - like attending cinemas, theatres, shows and musicals, etc. Joy-riding on the underground trains in London typified this form of socializing in the period under review - the days when Bing Crosby crooned his way into many hearts; when Glenn Miller's American Patrol pervaded the air waves; and when the forces darling Vera Lynn proclaimed in the most mellifluous tones that, when it was all over, " there'll be blue birds over the White Cliffs of Dover."

Those were the days when your uniform was a passport to many privileges. One only had to stand in the streets - uniform-clad - to be whisked away in a car, van or truck from one part of the country to the other without a penny being demanded. All this generosity abounded despite liberal issues of travel warrants to most UK destinations desired.

Cinemas - apart from providing shelter in inclement weather - soaked up huge chunks of time. There were periods when service people found themselves with a considerable amount of time to kill and quite often cinemas came to the rescue. One could easily have spent four, five or even more hours in the "pictures" or "flicks" as they were referred to in that period. The cinema had much to offer for, quite apart from two films - one long, the other short - there was an abundance of other entertainment, mainly news, predominantly about the War - for this was the pre-television era. One saw Movietone, Gaumont News, Pathe News, Paramount News and others, though not all at once. Then there was the cinema organist who, apparently, used to emerge from the "belly" of the building, dexterously playing the organ - arms and legs flailing to the amazement of the audience. Westindians always viewed such performances with wonderment. Having gone through the rounds of films, news and other entertainments - perhaps more than once, a substantial part of the day would have elapsed - very often leaving little or no time - after refreshments - for one's next appointment.

The theatre - likewise - accounted for devouring time and Westindians visited theatres in cities all over the country. However, it was in London that the greater numbers and variety were to be found. Towards the end of 1944 and the beginning of 1945, Peter Pan, Babes in the Wood, Uncle Vanya, Appointment with Death were all current.

Whether service people frequented London or not, one place visited at least once was the Nuffield Centre - that wonderful seat of entertainment situated in Wardour Street, donated to the services by William Morris (Lord Nuffield) who made his money in the production of the Morris Car. Thousands of service people (including Westindians) who were in the forces visited the Centre - many on more than one occasion - where there was always a variety of entertainment for a large part of each day. It was a favourite venue for arranging to meet people and many lost friends were re-found there. In the 1960s the whole of the Nuffield foundation was sold off and the funds invested in Service Establishments - including the Union Jack Club, Waterloo, London, which sheltered many servicemen during and after the War.

Westindian servicewomen - who seemed to have suffered none of the unpleasantness experienced by their male counterparts - adored the Nuffield Centre, finding every pretext to visit. Of the three servicewomen featured in this book, Esther Armagon, Carol Campbell and Norma Best, all were regular visitors to the Centre. Asked why the women favoured the Centre to such an extent, Norma Best says:

> "Well with many of us scattered around the country, the Nuffield Centre was the ideal place for us to meet to share the enjoyment."

Esther Armagon attended many dances and tea-parties, the cinema, theatre and musicals. One story she remembers and likes to relate happened when she was stationed on a prisoner of war camp in Wiltshire, working in the office there and allowed to speak to the POWs. One German ex-pilot used to make the most exquisite leather hand-bags and she obtained one for her mother, paying for it in Woodbine cigarettes!

Carol Campbell lived life to the full, indulging in private study, cycling, swimming, tennis, dancing in Darlington and, when on camp in Pontefract, Yorkshire and at the Hammersmith Palais. When in London she also recalls seeing shows like "Oklahoma" and "Annie Get Your Gun".

END OF HOSTILITIES; DEMOB

The end of the War was signified by two major civic events, the first being 'Victory in Europe' day, which occurred on 8th May 1945. VE day proclaimed the defeat by the Allied Forces over Hitler, Mussolini and the fascist forces. On that day a large victory parade was held in London. Stanley Hodges states that quite a few of his fellow servicemen were invited to take part in this parade. For him, no invitation was received, and he had "no regrets" about this after the treatment he and other Westindians had been subjected to. Robert Murray was also not in the VE day parade, although he takes a slightly different view of his exclusion from this event, stating that he:

> "... wasn't one of the fortunate ones to be on the parade."

He observed the whole parade as a spectator.

Ivor De'Souza remembers all work stopping, in terms of flying, and individuals indulging in parties, competitions and games on VE day. On that day he was actually in hospital after cutting his knee on some glass playing football the day before. However, this only slightly dampened down the euphoria of the occasion for him:

> ".... they took me to the hospital and the next day they had a great celebration and there I was in hospital with my foot in a bloody big plaster. They came across about five o'clock with bottles of whisky and so on and we all thoroughly enjoyed ourselves, although I felt such a fool in hospital."

The second major civic event occured on August 15th, 1945 with the surrender of Japan after the dropping of the atomic bombs on Hiroshima (August 6th) and Nagasaki (August 9th). 'Victory in Japan' day, otherwise known as VJ day, was in effect to herald a phase of transition for the Westindian servicemen. Stanley Hodges looks back:

> "It actually took maybe another six months or so before the end of

emergency was announced and before demob and repatriation started."

The Westindian servicemen were faced with a number of options. They could terminate their military service in the RAF and either settle in Britain or be repatriated to their respective countries. One Westindian ex-serviceman reminds:

> "...our period of service was ending because we all volunteered for the duration of the War and the War was finished. It's not like, say, the English boys who were in for as long as they kept them, and they kept some two or three years afterwards. We were essentially volunteers."

For James Moore's, return to England was essentially a return home as he was now domiciled in England, while Robert Murray decided to settle in Britain and enter civilian life. He states, about the decision to stay in England, that:

> "I found myself in two minds and one mind dominated the other with regards to staying. You see, because I saw, in my brief stay, so many opportunities in England that I thought it would be foolish to go back with nothing when all these facilities were in England. However I still longed for home. Indeed it presented a great dilemma: should one return home as empty headed as one arrived in the UK or should one stay and seek learning?"

Hence, for him, the experience he had gained of Britain and, in particular, of England during the War, had not curtailed his ambition of wanting to "better himself," nor had it diminished his desire to succeed in whatever he pursued and the more he thought about it, the more he became convinced that staying to gain knowledge and experience was the right course. So he stayed primarily to pursue a course in accountancy. Stanley Hodges also opted to stay in Britain after the War for similar reasons, stating that:

> ".... I felt I still had a better chance of improving my lot in England rather than going home at that particular time."

Ulric Cross recalls that the decision whether to stay or leave Britain was purely an individual one, with there being no policy concerning this issue at the time:

"There were no grounds, as far as the Colonial Office was concerned, to refuse to resettle people in the UK or to repatriate. Anybody who wanted to settle in Britain would be entitled to do so. At that time, of course, there was no question of an immigration policy. If you wanted to settle you just did so; if you wanted to go back home you went. The choice was entirely an individual's choice."

Later the Nationality Act of 1948 was to give individuals from the colonies the right to claim British citizenship.

Robert Murray states that the Westindian servicemen to whom he was welfare officer at Strubby in Lincolnshire were adamant about wanting to return to their island homes in the Caribbean. He recalls their vociferous demands which expressed their desperation to be repatriated:

".... they kept on to me, pestering me, saying, 'we want to go home'....I will never forget that period. Some boys would cry about missing their parents, their relatives and their girlfriends .... I used to get on to the Air Ministry to see that these boys were put onto what they called a draft to be sent home. They gave me so much trouble and some kept on and on. Then gradually they were drafted to go to different camps for onward transportation to their own countries whether it be Jamaica, or Trinidad, or Barbados, or wherever."

With a lot of other service people from various parts of the then British Commonwealth and Empire clamouring to go home, such as New Zealanders, Canadians, Indians and Africans, there was some shortage of available ships, hence the delay in getting Westindian servicemen home. Ulric Cross, who worked in the Colonial Office, was extensively involved in the repatriation of Westindians and claims, together with Robert Murray's account, that the majority of Westindian servicemen wanted to return home. Nevertheless, departures suffered further delay because:

".... there was the question of arranging not only transport for them back to the Westindies but also officers to accompany them."

For James McKenzie, Gerry Smith, Tony Daley and Athleston Holder, repatriation was to be a short-lived experience as they soon were to return to settle in Britain. Alternatively, the Westindian servicemen could have extended their time in the RAF. Gerald Beard and Stanley Hodges were two servicemen who committed themselves to another term of duty in the RAF. Gerald Beard signed on for four years, while Stanley Hodges signed on for a further three years. During this time all servicemen were given a two month period to decide whether they wanted to return to their respective countries or stay in the UK. This period was known as 'demob leave'. Stanley Hodges describes his post-War experience in the forces as one in which he was constantly posted to several stations around the country and remembers it in terms of two distinct phases:

> "The first year or so things moved fast. We were always on the road out of camp transporting surplus war materials, mainly surplus bombs and other ammunition. This activity at times could be somewhat dangerous as a mishap among a convoy could prove disastrous. Nevertheless we enjoyed the challenge."

In contrast to this experience he also relates:

> "The second half of my extended service wasn't going too well. The War was over, so obviously there would be a change in attitude, a change in thinking, a change in planning and rebuilding. As far as I was concerned service life had become a bore. All we seemed to be doing was painting walls and paths, washing and polishing lorries, etc, what is generally known as Bull, when I'd rather be doing something really constructive, really active than pretending to be. The Military activity process did not appeal any longer to me whereas we were made to do things just to keep us active, to keep us going, not for any particular reason."

Before leaving the armed services the Westindian servicemen could attend college courses if they wanted to which would usually last between six months and a year. Robert Murray explains the purpose of these courses:

> "The Colonial Office awarded courses to some of the ex-servicemen to fit them out for going back home. This was for those who didn't go back right away. They were known as the 'Colonial Office rehabilitation courses.' Some people would, for example, want to be engineers, farmers, carpenters, accountants, lawyers or such like, and they could get training depending on what was offered."

128

His recollections concerning the allocation of courses are in agreement, to some extent, with the experiences of most of those who received short-term courses, feeling that they were hard-done by:

> ".... you could select but they would say to you that this is what we have on offer. Mainly, these were things that they did in the Westindies like baking bread, agriculture, carpentry and joinery, that sort of thing. But when one came to higher courses like accountancy, they were very slow to award unless you could prove that you could maintain and, in the end, be successful with the course. My own feelings were that the higher your rank in the Air Force, the higher your course or the wider your choice."

James McKenzie, Robert Murray and Athleston Holder all gained places on these courses. Robert Murray was able to get on the course that he wanted, which was accountancy. However Athleston Holder was not so fortunate. His remarks on the allocation of courses echo the disappointment and betrayal that many Westindian servicemen were to experience over this issue:

> ".... they were supposed to fit me out for civilian life. I was temporarily released to enter Leicester Technical College, learning boot and shoe making. That was the choice forced on me. I wanted to be a mechanical engineer but such was not to be."

With the ending of the War the Westindian servicemen's careers in the RAF were terminated by their going through a de-militarization process termed "demobilization," otherwise known as "demob". This entailed the service personnel returning all weapons and other military hardware, returning their military uniforms and being given alternative clothes, which in most cases was a badly-fitting suit, and receiving their last service payment. Before actual demob occurred all the servicemen were given eight weeks demob leave which Robert Murray describes as being "like a honeymoon period" before finding a job. Hence de-militarization was the severing ritual by which the servicemen departed from the military life and re-entered civvy street. For some servicemen this event was highly significant as the comment by Adrian Neysnich, who was in the RAF since 1941, states:

129

"I wasn't demobbed in England because of unfortunate circumstances.... something to do with the government in Jamaica at the time, I think."

In the comments that followed this statement, Adrian Neysnich reveals a sense of betrayal and resentment about where and with whom he shared this event. In many respects his comment reveals that he felt he was sharing the glory of a war victory with others who had not actively taken part in its achievement:

"We were placed along with the Caribbean regiment.... but when they came, the War was already over. When the War was over we were sent back to Jamaica with their regiment, so I was demobbed in Jamaica with them."

A large number of Westindian servicemen were demobbed in Britain. They were then either repatriated to the Caribbean, as Ulric Cross was, or left to fend for themselves in Britain. Those who had obtained a high officer rank, like their white counterparts, retained that rank for life and were entitled to be addressed accordingly. This was the case for Ulric Cross who at the end of the War was a Squadron Leader and the highest ranking Westindian RAF serviceman. To this day he is still referred to as Squadron Leader Cross.

What lay in store for the Westindian servicemen when leaving the RAF and settling in the U.K. Robert Murray summed up as follows:

".... the biggest battle for survival was to come, but that is another story."

A story that will be unravelled in the following chapter.

ENTRY INTO CIVVY STREET

The Westindies, Guyana, Belize are cosmopolitan in the make-up of their population. There are all shades and colours of people emanating from a miscellany of nationalities - eg. blacks, whites, Chinese, Syrians, French, Portugese, Spanish, the indigenous native Amer-Indians, now in diminishing numbers. While in Guyana and Trinidad and Tobago, Indians from India constitute a substantial part of the inhabitants. Indeed such is the diversity in the composition of the population in that sphere of the world, producing a wide variety of pigmentation, that Bernard Shaw once described Jamaica as a land of "pink men." These nationalities and different shades of colour were represented within the Westindian contingents that were in the armed services during the War. In due course these shades were to have an important influence on these service personnel's experiences after the War.

Individuals with white complexions were the progeny of Europeans who settled in the Caribbean years gone by without inter-marrying. These white or 'near-white' Westindians were readily accepted and integrated quickly within the indigenous population in Britain without any difficulty as is revealed:

> "They strolled into accommodation and jobs quite easily. One recalls two fair-skinned Westindians, Jocobs and Joseph, both of whom were snapped up in college for accountancy positions before their exam results were known."

Other than their accents, these Westindians were indistinguishable from the indigenous population as their physical appearance was similar.

> "On the other hand the dark or darker skinned Westindians did not fare so well, particularly in the field of accommodation and jobs: for it is in these two basic aspects of life which a man must enjoy success if he is to retain reasonable peace of mind."

These service personnel, stripped of RAF protection and left to fend for themselves in a hostile, somewhat alien, environment now came up against the harsh realities of the denial of two of the basic necessities. For most of the non-white Westindians, now ex-service personnel, a dehumanizing process began. This situation came as a great shock to most of the Westindian ex-servicemen - many of whom had hailed from middle-class backgrounds and, being in the RAF, had been insulated until now; for whatever your white counterpart thought of you, he was constrained by RAF discipline, by King's Rules and Air Council's Regulations and last, but not least, by the Colonial Office. With all this protection gone, the boys were "Thrown to the wolves!". Gerald Beard succinctly expounds:

> "It's when the War finished they would make us think as if we didn't come to help them fight the War. Well, they actually turned on us after the War, saying 'the War is over now, we don't want you'. In fact, they still don't want us now. In the Air Force we did not come up against a lot of prejudice because we were secluded. We didn't have to go looking for a job, we didn't have to go and look for accommodation ...... but once you came out in civilian life you had to come up against them. You had to find a job and find a place to live and that sort of thing ..... we found a lot of prejudice."

Gerald Beard was one of those who went home to Jamaica at the end of the War and then returned to Britain. However, he did not find return very welcoming, prompting him to say:

> "If I knew it was such a situation I wouldn't have come back at all...let's put it this way, we helped them in their War. And I think if you help somebody in difficult times, I think it's only natural for them to show some appreciation in return. But they didn't. The very people whom you helped in their troubles... (gave the impression at times that) .... if they got the opportunity they would cut your throat."

Pasteur Irons concurs with Gerald Beard's view of how black servicemen were originally regarded and the distinction between civilian and military life:

> "Whatever treatment we received while in the RAF was nothing compared with our treatment in civvy street. Whatever the establishment thought of you in the Air Force, they were confined to rules and regulations. And after all we were all in England to help with

132

the War effort. With the War now ended and we out of uniform, it soon became clear that the Westindians were not required."

So for the Westindian ex-servicemen their Battle of Britain began with "demob."

Some of the Westindian servicemen had gone back to the Caribbean and were never to return to Britain to settle. One such individual, Ulric Cross, was to live a very fruitful and successful life. He had returned to live on the island of Trinidad and was a judge of the Court of Appeal. He also spent some time assisting other RAF ex-service personnel adjust and re-settle into civilian life in the Caribbean. With there being many thousands of former groundcrew personnel living in the Caribbean there was plenty of work for him to do. On retirement he became the Chairman of the Law Commission of Trinidad and Tobago, a position which brings him to England once a year. Adrian Neysnich was another serviceman that returned to Jamaica where he worked as a stationery engineer. He resided in Jamaica with his family until 1969 after which he went to live in America.

As stated previously, a number of the Westindian ex-servicemen who opted to be repatriated to the Caribbean returned to Britain. James McKenzie, George Powe, Athleston Holder, Tony Daley, Gerry Smith, Gerald Beard and Norma Best were amongst those who went back to the Caribbean but later elected to come back to Britain. Athleston Holder and Gerald Beard recalled what prompted them to return to Britain. Athleston Holder returned to Britain after spending eleven years in Jamaica where he managed a business until its failure in 1960. Gerald Beard suffered a similar fate and returned to Britain in 1949. He says:

> "I was doing cabinet making. But I'd just opened a shop, bought a large amount of lumber and other materials and started, well, me and a friend. But we were unsuccessful, for we found that everyone wanted credit."

Consequently, for these individuals the experience of Britain during the War contrasted with their post-War experience in the Caribbean, resulting in their believing, even with all the problems they had encountered, that Britain offered more opportunity and a degree of security.

Another returnee to Jamaica after the war was Billy Strachan - whose service career glowed with success and who enjoyed a brilliant war-time experience. Nevertheless, such success in the UK during the war failed to be reflected in his native land, where he was offered the same Civil Sevice post in the same grade (3) at which he had left when he departed for England in 1940. Needless to say, he declined it, and when he failed to procure a job which interested him, he set sail for the UK with Joyce, whom he'd met in Blackpool and was now his wife, with his children.

"I was bitterly disillusioned, and felt I could do much better in England. So we returned after only 15 months and I found immediate success, becoming Education Committee Clerk to Middlesex County Council."

Norma Best's account reveals that for some of the ex-service personnel their return route back to Britain was not direct. After serving three years in the ATS from 1944 to September 1947, she undertook a two year college course, at the end of which she returned to her native Belize (then British Honduras). There at a dance in 1951 she met her future husband - Chief Petty Officer R. Best - who was based there at the time. Following his posting to Sri Lanka (then Ceylon), she joined him there in 1954 when they were married. At the end of his military service they both returned to the UK, where they have remained ever since. She mothered three daughters who bore her five grandchildren.

James Moore was to win his battle in Britain for acceptance within the community eventually, even though the situation within the workplace had not changed drastically. His daughter recalls that his post-War experience of gaining employment was not too dissimilar from what he encountered before the Second World War.

"After the War he took his demob so we figured he was going to get a job now. When...(he went to the) ...employment office and they called up, I think it was a place called Netherfield or Colwick in Nottingham, and they told them they had a man there who was as black as the ace of spades, and to give him a job. Anyway, he went there and he got the job but there was still a lot of prejudice ...... he never was late and he would never take a day off, even if he was probably dying and if he needed a day off, he wouldn't take it for fear of losing his job. He did get sick very badly and so he took three days off, sent in a doctor's certificate but by the end of that week he was feeling much better so he decided to go down and pick up his pay cheque. Well, when he went to work on the Monday morning he felt fine and they fired him because he had been off. They said, if you were well enough to come and pick up your pay cheque you should have been at work."

Nevertheless after the War he was accepted by the community he lived in. In fact, he was viewed as one of the pillars of the community:

"Except for the War period when he was abroad he always lived in Nottingham. He was very well known, very well liked. Funny the white people around where we lived, the odd one or two, would come to him if they wanted to know something, they would come to him for his help, to assist them with whatever it was. They just had faith in him, I guess. He had been there for so many years and I guess they saw that he was a clean-living man and everything."

George Powe's experience illustrates some of the problems that Westindian ex-servicemen faced. He originally opted to be repatriated to Jamaica where he stayed for nine months. He had intended to join the Merchant Navy but returned to England because he was 'weak-willed' and succumbed to his friend's persuasive powers. On returning to England he found himself in a catch-22 situation:

"I found I couldn't get a job because a lot of employers said that I was not in the union, and when I approached the union, they said they couldn't give me a card because I didn't have a job, so I went to the dole office. I didn't get a penny."

James McKenzie also returned to Britain after a spell in Jamaica and recalls that:

"On one occasion, looking for a job, I was told they were saving jobs for their own Englishmen so I had to take any job until I found something suitable."

This, for some ex-servicemen, meant that they had to attempt to gain

135

employment by using the trades they used, to good effect, in the War effort. For instance, Athleston Holder's first employment was similar to that which he performed in the Air Force. He worked at Foston Army Depot, near Derby for three months. Stanley Hodges was one who also, reluctantly, pursued this course of action in order to gain a job.

> "My experience again in Derby was somewhat frustrating because having gone through an experience in the Air Force as a motor transport driver I didn't imagine myself as a truck driver for the rest of my life. However, it was the only thing I knew then. So I ventured out seeking employment as a truck driver. After a week or two making personal and written applications I was unable to get employment as a driver."

As stated in an earlier chapter, some of the ex-servicemen went on courses so as to "fit them out" for civilian life. After completing either college courses or training courses the Westindian ex-servicemen should have been in a better position to gain employment. Stanley Hodges was one of those who chose to pursue the invitation to be trained for a trade. In attempting to gain employment the ex-servicemen would seek assistance from what was called the "Labour Exchange," the equivalent of the present day Social Security Department. The Labour Exchange had a department that was set up to cater exclusively for ex-service personnel. Stanley Hodges went to this department of the Labour Exchange and enquired about taking part in the government training scheme that was being run at the time for ex-service personnel. On confronting the clerk in charge he recalls being told that the qualifications he had were not sufficient for him to begin training as a refrigeration engineer. He continues:

> "I was very disappointed but I was informed that the only other two jobs available were for a wood machinist or a shoe maker; I decided to opt for the wood machinist."

Pasteur Irons encountered a similar experience to Stanley Hodges, in that the trade he actually wanted to go into was engineering but he was not too disgruntled in settling for life as a coal miner since the income he received was better than that of an engineer.

The courses and training many Westindian service personnel undertook were at the Colonial Office's discretion as Robert Murray relates:

> "Indeed it was often stated that the courses were not a right, but only a goodwill gesture."

These courses were meant to benefit both the service personnel and their home countries. For this reason there was no demob prior to going on the courses or training. All service personnel undertaking such courses were merely temporarily released from the RAF for the duration of the course, and at the completion, returned to the RAF to be repatriated, or if requested, to be demobbed in the UK.

It was never envisaged that individuals from the Caribbean who served in the UK would stay or even want to stay in the UK, where there was a surplus of qualified and able people in all trades and professions. Although officially there was no policy of forced repatriation there was an expectation that the Westindian ex-servicemen would return to the Caribbean. Some people were repatriated to countries of their choice, for example quite a few went directly to the USA and Canada, as in those days few immigration restrictions existed. With there being no official forced repatriation policy, covert attempts where made to pressurise the ex-service personnel to return to their own countries in spite of the fact that all the Caribbean ex-service personnel were British citizens. These secretive attempts to persuade individuals to return to their home countries were veiled under the pretext that they were needed under the rehabilitation programmes. One ex-serviceman who experienced such coercion, elucidates:

> "When my course ended I wanted to stay in England to acquire further qualifications, but the Colonial Office did their best to dissuade me. They kept telling me: 'Well, you can't stay here! You must go back and help your own people, after all you did sign to stay for the duration of the present emergency,' and this and that. However when they saw I was adamant, particularly when I pointed out that I was a British subject, I was entitled to domicile in the UK and they couldn't legally send me home, they desisted from further pressuring, so I stayed."

At any rate those who did such courses seemed to fare no better than those who opted to look for work straight away. Stanley Hodges recalled going for a job and being rejected offhandedly by the employers, even after completing a nine month training course as a wood machinist at a government training centre. He was sent to a particular firm in Long Eaton which had advertised for workers at the centre. He continues:

> "This establishment already knew that I was coming as I was introduced to that firm as a trainee wood machinist. On my personal appearance the manager looked at my card, had a good look at me, and he just said, 'Sorry, you're no good to us.' There was very little I could do. I came away feeling very down-hearted but nevertheless determined to get work in that particular field."

The union card referred to was essential if one sought a job in a trade involving a union. It represented one's passport to a job but possessing a union card before commencing a job was, in most cases, rigidly applied to Westindians. It had been known for whites to start jobs without cards and produce them days or even weeks later. Most Westindians never enjoyed such luck. Two examples have just been given in which one Westindian - George Powe - had no card and failed to obtain a job; another - Stanley Hodges - who was turned down flat even though he possessed one. So most Westindians found themselves on the losing side whatever the rules.

Yet the proverbial exception to the rule operated even then. George Haynes went for a job at British Celanese and was most surprised when a letter arrived inviting him to an interview:

> "The bloke there was reluctant to start me without a union card. I went round to the ETU (Electrical Trades Union), got a card and started work as an Improver - not as an electrician. After three months, the foreman came round and told me I was upgraded to Skilled Electrician. One day they wanted a shop steward and I was asked to do it. I accepted and became the very first black shop steward in that firm - a position I held until I retired."

Laurie Phillpotts did a course at Leeds Technical College after leaving the RAF. His interest was printing, he took the City and Guilds finals in Linotype and Typesetting. He also attended

Nottingham Technical College, where he got to know Trade Union Officials through whom he obtained his union card. Leaving Nottingham in 1959, he went to Welwyn Garden City, then he applied to London Society of Compositors and worked with a commercial firm for a few years before joining Fleet Street as a Glass Hand (casual work) while waiting to become fully-fledged: "As a Westindian, one had to be very diplomatic," he states. He worked in Fleet Street for 15 years before taking voluntary retirement after obtaining satisfactory terms around 1988.

After visiting the Labour Exchange, Robert Murray recalls encountering constant snubs when seeking a job. He would often be told that he was too qualified for a position and, when he stated that he was willing to take a lower wage for the job, his offer would be rejected on the grounds that it would be unfair to do so. He further recalls, in some detail, one incident that was to cause him to contemplate going back to Guyana because of the "frustrating" and "depressing" barriers that he needed to confront:

> "I'd never forget being sent to a place in Holborn, London, and I was standing there for what seemed to me about half an hour. It must have been longer. It was a vast office with dozens of people moving about, and nobody apparently seemed to take any notice of me as I stood with this bit of paper in my hand that I got from the Forces Exchange. I thought, should I introduce myself? But they seemed so busy. After about half an hour a man came up to me, I could see he was annoyed, and asked gruffly, almost impersonally; 'What's that man waiting for? What do you want!?' just like that. Then I showed him this paper.
>
> 'Who sent you here? I don't want anybody. I'm going to get in touch with these people and tell them not to send any more of you people. If I knew that you people came from there I would not use that agency. We don't have any vacancy!'"

In response to ordeals like this, the majority of Westindian ex-servicemen would move from one city to another in search of work. George Powe moved from Liverpool to Birmingham and then finally to Nottingham. Stanley Hodges originally opted to settle in Derby but later moved to Nottingham, while Gerald Beard's first choice was to resettle in London. He then moved on to Manchester and finally ended up residing in Nottingham. Hence the proverbial bike was much in use by Westindian ex-servicemen.

Westindian ex-servicemen selected cities as suitable places to attempt to settle in on the basis of a number of factors. The most obvious reason for moving to any city was whether the chances of gaining employment were high. George Powe affirmed, he moved from Liverpool to Birmingham because:

> "I heard that you could get jobs in Birmingham and three of my colleagues said, 'let's go to Birmingham.'"

While in Liverpool he observed that:

> ".... in spite of there being a demand for labour all over the country, the majority of blacks were unemployed in Liverpool."

He described the atmosphere of Liverpool at the time as being "very tense":

> "There were two reasons for this: the level of unemployment among the blacks and the assumption that blacks only went with white women because they wanted to put them on the streets. Those were the kinds of arguments that were being put forward, so the blacks were no good and they wanted to get them out of the town. So, there was a tendency to attack blacks for those two reasons."

In many respects the black people in Liverpool were being used as scapegoats for the plight that everyone was in, for there was also a number of white people unemployed as well.

Having a friend or relative in the city was also a consideration for the Westindian ex-servicemen when selecting a place to re-locate themselves. Not only did these contacts offer them social support, but in some cases they would offer them lodgings. A final reason for electing to go to one city rather than another was whether any black community existed there and what knowledge they had of the city. For instance, Gerald Beard moved to Nottingham mainly for the latter reason, in that he had visited Nottingham regularly when given leave from his duties in the RAF. Stanley Hodges first opted for Derby because:

> "At the time my friend had regularly visited Derby and had friends

there among the local people. We thought that, as this was an industrialized town, it would be much easier for us to obtain work and training than anywhere else we could think of."

The Westindian ex-servicemen encountered some blatant racism even when visiting the government-run Labour Exchanges. At times they would receive a frosty reception from the person behind the counter, as George Powe recalls:

"The normal thing was that when you went to the window a girl would open the window .... she would say ....' oh, we don't employ niggers' or 'we don't want any labourers today,' without asking you what you'd come for."

Actually, to a lesser extent, white ex-servicemen themselves also faced problems in gaining employment as he continues to recall:

"As a matter of fact, the white young ex-servicemen had some very bad experiences, when they came out of the forces. Employers were saying that they were lazy, they were not accustomed to work, the service had spoilt them and didn't give them jobs. At the same time they were in a better position than blacks to get jobs. It's like the British people had made an about-turn. The day before they were hugging you, kissing you, patting you on the back, apart from the fight that I told you about. Immediately after the war you were nothing but lazy ba****ds. That attitude came over very strongly too."

Only with persistence and strength of character were the Westindian ex-servicemen, especially those with darker complexions, able to gain employment. As Pasteur Irons states, in his search for a better job:

"I got on my bike, I couldn't afford the bus fare, and I went round the different local collieries. Everywhere the door was shut in my face, no, no, no."

The constant effect of being rejected in pursuit of employment and the resolve to succeed was taking its toll. Becoming frustrated with the situation, he recalls clearly:

".... being married with children I was desperate for work. I went for a

141

job at one ironworks. I passed the test, tried everything but they turned me down. Then I went to another well-known company. They told me to wait while they interviewed all the ex-prisoners of war, the very people we left our homelands to fight against. It was then more than at any time I regretted staying in England, for nothing could be more humiliating than my early job-seeking experiences. Foot-slogging, looking for jobs everyday became tedious and depressing. I sometimes became scared; scared not of people, but of being rejected and of my aggressive retaliation. But what could I do? I had to carry on, I dared not lose hope."

George Powe states:

"…. you find that you would go to, say, ten or twenty places, and you might be lucky to be interviewed for one of those jobs."

It must be remembered that there could be no excuse, no reasonable grounds for such refusals, as those were the days of over-full employment.

Even after a competent interview there was no guarantee of a post at the end. Again one of George Powe's experiences illustrates this fact and clearly demonstrates white men's concern about black men's relationships with white women:

"One of my worst experiences was when I went for a job in Aston, and I was invited into the director's office. He asked me if I wanted something to drink, I said 'anything.' He asked me if I'd like a drink of spirits, I said, 'oh yes,' and he brought me some brandy, and he called one of his staff to make coffee. I had coffee, I thought I'd at least got the job now. I was really chuffed that there was a job coming. At the end of it he said, 'Well, you know Mr Powe I am very sorry, but I will not give you a job.' Before I'd asked him why he decided to explain. He said, 'You see you are a very intelligent man and I will help you as much as I can, if you are short of funds come and see me and I will give you some money, anytime.' So I waited for him to continue and he said, 'You see, one of the things is, we employ women here.' Honestly! I could have dropped through the floor. He said, 'We employ white women, and if I employ you it's obvious that you will have to move around with women and the other workers wouldn't like it', so I told him to 'f**k off'. He offered me five pounds, and five pounds at that time was quite a lot of money; I refused his five pounds. That was one occasion when I thought I was going to get a job."

Robert Murray suffered a not too dissimilar experience as George Powe when, armed with a 'piece of paper' from the Forces Labour Exchange, he went to a firm in Oxford Street, London. "You will be alright there," the man behind the counter of the Labour Exchange confided to him. "They seem really nice people," he was assured. Robert Murray tells his story:

"I made my way up a flight of stairs. The firm required a bookkeeper with a good general education and with the appropriate bookkeeping qualifications, or equivalent, to be in charge of a small accounts section. I immediately fancied my chances after seeing a tall man at the top of the stairs offering me a welcoming hand-shake. His face was bathed in smiles.

'Welcome, my brother,' he said to me jovially. He said his name was Drummond, John Drummond, and asked if I had much difficulty finding the place.

'No,' I replied, feeling optimistic, 'none at all.'

'Good,' he said, 'let's go inside.'

He led me into a well-arranged office and offered me a seat. He had an oval-shaped face on which a smile sat easily. He said:

'We are a small family firm and have been going since the turn of the century, you know. We are all Christians here, are you a Christian Mr Murray? I come from a deeply religious family - the Plymouth Brelkren. I myself was preaching on the streets at the age of twelve.'

'Yes,' I said, 'I come from a Christian background.'

This was the nearest I'd come to a job, and I thought that something must be at the end of the interview. After all the boss was a Christian who talked at great length, although about everything except the job. When at last he asked for my qualifications I gladly handed them to him. He studied them with great interest then he groaned:

'Hnnnn-quite impressive. Of course you're far too over qualified for our small firm. Our pay offer of £7 is far too modest for you.'

I told him I was willing to accept that, considering it to be a good wage at the time. He turned his head aside and veered off in another direction, talking about religion again. This was all very well but I went there for a job and not to talk about religion. Although in a way I was pleased, feeling that religion would make me more amenable to him and hence ensuring me a job.

However, time was marching on. 'But the job' I reminded.

'Oh yes,' he said, 'the job,' he muttered. Then he continued with the most extraordinary suggestion I have ever heard in such a situation. 'Let's kneel down and pray, my brother.' He called me his brother so often I almost began to believe we were blood relations or something.

Just then, there was a tap on the door and a young lady entered with a tray two cups of tea and some biscuits. 'Thank you, Dorothy,' he said without looking up at her.

'Come on my brother', he urged, 'let's indulge in a little prayer - works wonders in times like these.' So down we knelt and he started. Now I was not averse to prayers, in fact I rather liked them. But I felt that there was a time and place for that sort of thing. Mr Drummond went on and on, praying away, long and interminable at times, working himself up into a frenzy like some demented lay-preacher at a revivalist meeting! Of course, one didn't mind it if there was going to be a silver lining in the form of a job.

I suddenly got it into my head that this man was simply stalling for time. I decided enough was enough, so when he paused for a change of air, I exulted 'Amen! Amen!' and got up. Mr Drummond seemed somewhat disconcerted as he rose. 'Amen,' he repeated. We'd been down on our knees for so long that the tea by now was stone cold and I'd almost forgotten what I'd gone there for in the first place.

Feeling all this was somewhat pointless, I put the question to him point blank!

'So am I going to get the job or not?'

He assumed the posture of prayer bowing his head and said, 'my brother....'

I thought to myself, 'I wish he'd stop calling me 'brother'' as I was positive he didn't mean it, and it was a biological impossibility, anyway.

'You know,' he said, 'my brother, it's not as simple as that.'

'Why not?' I said, astonished.

'You see, my brother, my partner is away on holiday and I can do nothing without him.'

'But the job notice at the Exchange said nothing about waiting for a partner, it just said, wanted immediately!' I continued. 'Neither did you mention about a partner until now.'

For the first time since our encounter, Mr Drummond stalled. I now came to the painful realization there was no job for me. The whole thing was a complete and utter waste of time. How could I have been so gullible? I thought to myself, 'You lying hound! Call yourself a Christian?' As I slowly made my way down the stairs he had the audacity to howl after me, 'Don't lose heart, my brother. Don't lose heart, we'll pray for you,' as though that would put food in my belly."

For Robert Murray this episode drove home the true nature of Britain's view of him - not as a lost son but more as an expendable resource:

"Outside in Oxford Street the traffic was grinding away and people, the

144

ever present hordes, kept milling about. With the name of Drummond still drumming in my head, songs from my boyhood days started to flood into my mind - 'Children of the Empire,' 'Rule Britannia,' 'Land of Hope and Glory,' and I couldn't help thinking, 'I own no land, there is no glory, and certainly no bloody hope!' Then, drumming in time to the traffic one word kept piercing my mind - deception, deception, deception!!!"

Once given an opportunity to work, the Westindian ex-servicemen were at the whims and caprices of the employers and hence would be sacked for trivial matters. Stanley Hodges was sacked for refusing to sweep up rubbish, cleaning up, which he felt was outside the scope of his job. One incident that George Powe experienced and which resulted in him getting sacked, reverberated with the same undercurrents familiar to most Westindian ex-servicemen:

"I got a job at a firm called Dowshall Illumination Engineers. I was working there as an Electrical Fitter and one of the members of staff in the office, a woman, apparently became very friendly. Sometimes she would bring me fruits and all these kinds of things and one day I was called into the office and I was told that they were giving me a fortnight's notice. So I asked, 'What have I done?' I was told the reason I got sacked was because I was too friendly with this woman, and because the men were complaining that I was talking to a white woman in the firm. Well, there were no black women there, and I was the only black person, so I was sacked because of that."

When such incidents occurred there was no redress from tribunals, or protection from trade unions at the time. In fact, as far as George Powe was concerned the unions were themselves not altogether blameless. The unions, according to Gerald Beard and Pateur Irons, restricted the opportunities open to black people. In Gerald Beard's case he was prohibited from getting a job and subsequently had to leave Manchester, because of his inability to obtain a work-card necessary to practice his trade in woodwork. In Pasteur Iron's case he was nearly prevented from using new equipment at his work place by the executive of the union. But in this case the local branch of the union intervened:

"They sent me on a course ... to go and learn this new machine ... the union had an agreement with the coal board firm that had just been nationalised that ... the best job must go to those that were British, not to foreigners ... They wanted the ... local branch of the ... union to implement the 1947 agreement. Myself and the other bloke, who was a Russian, but a naturalised Britisher, they wanted to take us off that job, but the local union told them we were British citizens."

Racism within the workplace was so prevalent that in one instance it caused a black ex-serviceman, in response to the abuse he faced, to leave his job, such was its intensity and persistence. George Powe left his electrical job after only four months. Why?

".... because I was asked all sorts of stupid questions, if I knew when I wanted a wash and all these kind of things because of my colour."

Gerry Smith encountered a similar situation, although hitherto he'd recalled experiencing neither prejudice nor discrimination. He, like many of his Westindian compatriots who had been in the Armed Services, opted to return to the Caribbean after the War, settling in Jamaica. He was working at the Westindian Sugar Company until, urged by Christian friends in England where both his church activities and organ playing would be welcomed, to return to Britain. On his return he found accommodation in Annerley, S.E. London, and a good job in West Croydon, Surrey. He also met his wife there. He worked in a chocolate factory for quite a while where, for the very first time, prejudice was to raise it's ugly head. Gerry Smith recalls that his charge-hand was retiring and:

"I was recommended by the foreman as being highly suitable to replace the charge-hand. He said to me: 'Don't mention it to anyone - I recommended you for that job, but the manager said, do you think I'd put a black man in charge of white people?' I was dumbfounded because I mixed with everyone, never had any problems with any of the men. As a result someone was transferred from another department who I had to train! I remained there for another two months and, as a matter of principle, I never did my job as well again. Even the manager himself found that things were not the same. I left shortly afterwards for a job in Derby."

Nearly all the Westindian ex-servicemen that returned to, or stayed in, Britain after the War, had done so in the expectation that greater opportunity was open to them in Britain than in the Caribbean, but the vast majority of these individuals were to be disappointed as to what they could attain within the labour market. Stanley Hodges opines:

> "It didn't seem accidental to us that blacks worked in iron foundries because obviously there was the racial tendency there, and I think that it was no use at the time saying that I was a draughtsman or technician or electrical engineer or something like that. I don't think we stood a chance of being employed in those particular fields, so it was obvious the menial jobs were the only jobs for us. You either took them or left them. We had no choice."

George Powe affirms:

> ".... there were patterns because we were only given the dirty jobs. Very few of us managed to get any decent jobs. As a matter of fact, out of the lot, I would say it was no more than about ten of us that were in any skilled work in Birmingham and there were chaps with good qualifications, with degrees and all these things. They had to sweep up."

Pasteur Irons's first job was in a factory making cardboard boxes in which his take-home pay, to support a wife and child, was £3 a week. He later managed to gain a well-paid job in Nottingham at Clifton Colliery, only by convincing the employer that he would stay there for some time.

Discrimination in the field of work in a period of over-full employment had the effect of demolishing both the confidence and morale of the ex-servicemen. Many of these were individuals who had made sacrifices and had given their all voluntarily only to be frustrated at every turn. Some of the ex-servicemen never secured the jobs they yearned for and subsequently had to settle for anything they could get. Eric Hudson and Alwyn Pindar were two ex-servicemen who were forced to adopt this ploy. Both originally preferred upholstery as their trade but neither found success in this field. Eric Hudson decided to go back to his native Jamaica in 1948, took a brief look at it, tried England again in 1949, departing once again from England to attempt to resettle in the United States but after two years he ran up against 'The McLaren Act' which forced him to return to the UK. Further attempts to procure employment in upholstery proved no more successful than previously, causing him to concede defeat. He then opted for a labourer's job in a chemical factory, followed by moulding in a rubber factory, then going back to work with Imperial Typewriters before finally settling at the Leicester City Council as a Youth and Community Worker after a college course. He stayed in that job for fifteen years until his retirement in 1993.

It took Alwyn Pindar two years to procure a union card in pursuit of a job in the upholstery trade but his long wait availed him nothing for, at his very first interview, he was told:

> "Your hands are too soft."

No further opportunities for work as an upholsterer presented themselves. In the end a friend got him a job as a store-keeper in the printing trade from which, having been made redundant, he tried taxi-driving. He says:

> "Not being your own boss was a handicap. Things were not as easy as all that. First, there was a test to be taken. Secondly, accidents occurred more often than one would have liked and insults were not infrequent. I once tried to help an elderly lady and, as soon as I stretched my hand out to assist her, she became distraught, shouting; 'Don't touch me! ... don't you touch me!'"

Vernon Hunte, Bob Roach, Owen Sylvester, Ron Hall and scores of others not mentioned here pounded the streets to no avail in search of jobs during the period under discussion.

Ronald Hall, previously mentioned as having made a very meteoric rise in rank in the RAF had changed his intended course from economics - which he was studying while in the service - to dentistry. He had joined the International Dental Federation, travelling around the world before embarking on his studies but he remains reticent about his experiences while in pursuit of his first job after qualifying in dentistry at Guys Hospital, London. It is, however, known that he suffered as badly as most other Westindian ex-servicemen, grinding down his shoe-leather to no avail for some considerable time. A dentist once told him that if he gave him a job and things didn't go well, he'd lose his practice after being in it for 20 years and he couldn't risk that. Yet, when asked how he fared in those early days, he would always grin, saying:

> "I never like such questions because black people like to hear you've been treated badly. Suffice to say that I've had my disappointments earlier on but I've survived. If you leave your country to settle in another, you've got to take what comes. It's no use moaning about it now."

This discrimination was not limited to employment, as it was generally known, but also extended its ugly tentacles to other fields, not least entertainment. Frank Holder, previously mentioned as having sung with many leading bands of the day including Lou Preager, Joe Loss, Andre Masseda, a Latin American Band, The Basil Holiday Band in Long Eaton Nottingham, winning many singing competitions whilst still in the RAF, found it difficult to land a permanent vocalist job immediately after the War.

Discrimination sometimes took a most peculiar form - as the time when Frank Holder entered for The King and Queen Stage Competition at the Lyceum Ballroom in The Strand, London. A victory would have greatly advanced his career. The Lyceum Ballroom sloped downwards from the stage and the floor happened to be crowded on that occasion. The judges were unable to see the faces of the competitors, only their backs, revealing their numbers which, in Holder's case, was number 10. His friend Les Howard, who was white and also a competitor, happened to glance over both judges' shoulders and saw number 10 written down as the winner. He immediately turned to Frank Holder and congratulated him. Frank Holder replied:

> "Let's wait for the announcement. I've had mind-changes before."

Sure enough, the official announcement, to the surprise and consternation of most present, made Les Howard the winner, with Frank Holder second, a result which Frank Holder took with some resignation. Obviously, the revelation of his colour resulted in the judges hasty reversal of their decision. Nothing could have convinced Frank Holder, together with a large part of the audience, otherwise. As it was, he had to be content with his second prize, part of which included a visit to Lime Grove Studios and being shown around by the well-known actor, Vincent Price. Frank Holder and Les Howard remain good friends and even today have a good laugh over the incident.

Months elapsed and Frank Holder was beginning to despair of ever procuring the career nearest and dearest to his heart - singing - when he received a telephone call from Leslie (Jiver) Hutchinson, a big band leader, whom he had previously met at Nottingham Baths. Hutchinson liked his singing and promised to be in touch with him. Of course, Holder had heard such promises before - all of which came to nought. Nevertheless, this telephone call - when it came - was quite productive as he started working with the first All-black Band which pleased him immensely. His career took off from there - as Jiver Hutchinson's Band was extremely popular at the time. He gained even more fame as a singer when he began to sing with the John Dankworth Orchestra. He remembers his first engagement at the Gaumont State, Kilburn. His first recording was 'Don't Blame Me.' Cleo Lane joined the band about one year later. While singing with the Johnny Dankworth Band, he met and helped a very young Shirley Bassey. Frank met and sometimes helped several singers, many of whom became household names such as Nat King Cole, Mat Munroe, Lena Horn. Frank became big in several countries - in Europe, Africa, Asia - and in 1956 he was voted among the top four vocalists in the UK by The Melody Maker, being placed above Dickie Valentine, Frankie Vaughn and Denis Lotis. Frank Holder is still soothing hearts with his mellifluous tones.

However, it would be remiss, hypocritical and disingenuous not to portray the other side of the coin. A few Westindians did get very good jobs without apparent difficulty. Two factors accounted for this, one being the law of averages; the other, good fortune.

One ex-serviceman remembers Basil Hines rushing into college one day, beaming from ear to ear and announcing that he'd just picked up a job as a bookkeeper, as easily as shelling peas;

> "'Man,' he grinned, 'you could knock me down with a feather when they said the job was mine.'

It was a remarkable success because, although he'd taken the intermediate exam the results had not yet been published.

'The first time,' he said, 'the very first time. I've never applied for a job before.' What's more, he was to start the following day! Such luck was beyond belief. All the other students were touching him all over for luck, they couldn't comprehend it! They never expected it! In fact, Basil himself couldn't have dreamt of it. He only saw the job advertised in the previous evening's paper and decided to chance his luck on the way to college the following morning. As it happened the job was advertised over a month before. They'd interviewed, drawn up a short list and made a final selection. A young man, who should have started that very morning, had telephoned to say he'd secured a better job and the firm was stuck. So along came Basil and bingo! He landed a job!"

When Billy Strachan landed a job with the Middlesex County Council immediately upon returning from his brief stay in Jamaica, he did not rest on his laurels, but embarked on a series of evenings and weekend studies - namely - accountancy and law. An extremely fast learner, he soon obtained the FCIS (Fellow of the Chartered Institute of Secretaries) exams and the LLB (Bachelor of Law) degree, becoming a barrister and was appointed Clerk to the Justices of Bow Street. He afterwards worked at the Inner London Magistrates Courts until given a permanent seat as the Senior Chief Clerk (West Central Division Clerkenwell and Hampstead Magistrate Court.

The recollections of Tony Daley, Norma Best, Godfrey Petgrave, Bill Henriques and Sidney Mathews reveal that some of the ex-service personnel had little difficulty in obtaining employment. For instance, Tony Daley was one of the Westindian ex-service personnel who went back to Jamaica when the War ended and returned in 1949. He states that he encountered no problems in obtaining his first job at a timber company in Nottingham. He left to train as a wood-machinist, returning afterwards as a skilled manual worker there for many years. Norma Best apparently encountered none of the problems in the field of employment experienced by the majority of Westindian ex-servicemen. She pursued a teaching career from 1965 which stretched for twenty-three years, the last twelve of which she was a head teacher.

Carol Campbell and Esther Armagon also experienced none of the traumas in procuring employment as the majority of the servicemen. Carol Campbell used an agency through which she always found satisfaction with jobs - even enjoying a position at the Conservative Central Office from 1973 to 1981, the last two being Thatcher Years. After the War Esther Armagon remained in the UK and trained as a nurse at Hammersmith Hospital, London. She then undertook further training as a midwife before returning to her native Jamaica where, not too happy with conditions there, she found herself back in the UK after only ten months, and started working at Lewisham Hospital, London, as a midwife shortly afterwards.

Godfrey Petgrave was temporarily released from the RAF to pursue a course in Edinburgh at the School of chiropody. He was recommended by the Head of the School in Edinburgh for a job in Nottingham, June 1949, to work in the general dispensary. He had an interview, got the job and stayed for twenty-nine years. He then applied for and got the post of Sector Chiropodist for the city to develop centres within the Health Service. He did this work for six years before leaving to start his own practice. He goes on to assert that his success was due entirely to being a professional and being under the guidance of the Edinburgh School of Chiropody which virtually insulated him from unemployment and job hunting.

Carl Brewster, on the other hand, who also studied chiropody at the Chelsea School of Chiropody and who was aware of Godfrey Petgrave through Association Journals, had a most dissimilar experience after qualifying. He remembers the problems that afflicted him in pursuit of a job as a black chiropodist. For him, it became a nightmare - far worse than he had imagined it to be when in training. He says:

> "Things got so desperate that I decided to work for myself - to be in charge of my own destiny. No longer would I depend on others to give me a job."

Bill Henriques, after a nine month electrical training course, claims he also easily obtained employment in Derby. He goes on to state that he had sent home to Jamaica for his qualifications confirming that he was an electrician, but before these had arrived he was ratified as a "fully-fledged electrician." He perceived his colour was not an issue in his gaining and staying in employment:

"My work was considered first class. Many were sacked, black and white, because they were incompetent. All they were interested in was that you could do the job. If you came up to scratch you were in; if not you were out!"

Sidney Mathews never experienced any protracted periods of unemployment and gained his first job in Long Eaton, Nottinghamshire, where he worked for three years. From there he went on to work at an iron foundry in Sandiarce, Nottinghamshire, for thirty-six years. It was while he was working in Long Eaton that Sidney Mathews met Vincent Miller, referred to elsewhere in this book as being responsible for highlighting the Jamaica branch of the RAF Association. Vincent Miller worked at this firm from 1949, became a foreman, and was still there in January 1987 when he died.

So, for some Westindian ex-service personnel the dreaded 'pangs' of discrimination and prejudice were experiences they hardly encountered.

Closely allied with the need to gain employment was that of finding accommodation, which presented another problem for the Westindian ex-servicemen. Robert Murray articulates the attitude that prevailed at that time:

"The accommodation in whole houses and flats virtually vanished and rooms ceased to exist in the few minutes it took an inquirer to walk round a corner. Heads would shake negatively and doors would be slammed violently in our faces. Notices warning, 'No wogs, niggers and dogs,' were not uncommon. One would be told, quite unashamedly, 'We don't want you 'ere'. The excuses came thick and fast: 'It's not me it's my husband,' or vice versa, or 'It's my lodgers,' 'It's my neighbours'."

These occurrences typified frequent experiences for some of the ex-service personnel. There were no race relation laws in those days, so people did what they liked with impunity.

"It was extremely annoying when it occurred - not to mention humiliating. It was all the more exasperating as one could do nothing about it, only walk meekly away, with head down and with pride severely damaged."

A typical encounter is here depicted:

"I rang and they told me to 'come round, the room was ready now.' I ran all the way and arrived in the twinkling of an eye. At the door a woman told me 'It's gone, just gone,' without a word of apology!"

He continues:

"I felt gutted! Gutted not simply because I didn't get the room but because I knew it was impossible for it to be let in such a short space of time. I knew it still existed and I felt so insulted and degraded!!! Unmanned!!!"

Pasteur Irons would never forget a Mrs Goodwin in a certain street in Nottingham telling him she had no rooms when the opposite was true, as a white chap went in and spoke to her and, as a result, she gave him a room. The next morning she tried to apologise but Pasteur Irons would have none of it. The damage was already done. The unavailability of accommodation to blacks in those days was almost total. Frank Holder remembers entertaining in a place called Thame in Scotland and at the end, in the small hours of the morning, the promoter mounting the stage to plead for accommodation for members of the 16-strong Leslie Hutchinson's All black Band. The plea was successful. People opened their front rooms to give them shelter for the night. It is difficult to visualize the amount of ignorance that existed in those days. The following morning one of the ladies who offered accommodation started to 'pat' cushions, saying to a few members:

"Come on, dears, rest your tails on these cushions." They all laughed.

Frank Holder states:

"This was no prejudice or insult, these people genuinely believed that all black people had tails."

On another occasion in Nottingham, while with the Johnny Dankworth Band, Frank said the hotelier took one look at him and decided he couldn't be accepted. Johnnny Dankworth made it abundantly clear that Frank Holder was a member of his band and if he had to go, they would all go; so said, so done. They all departed for another hotel. Something similar occurred in Norwich. In Grimsby, there was no problem with accommodation but the landlady apologised for:

> "Not having the proper foods - parched grass and a bit of Shrunken Heads."

Frank Holder - playing to the situation regretted the non-availability of such nutrition saying;

> "They would have gone down well with a bit of pepper and salt."

The unavailability of lodgings, whether for reasons of paucity or discrimination, was one of the factors why Gerald Beard left London. In fact, George Powe, on his first night in Birmingham, spent the whole night on the streets. Pasteur Irons describes the accommodation situation that existed for Westindian ex-service personnel then:

> "We lived in hostels. There was nowhere else to live, you see, and people wouldn't give you anywhere. Westindians were buying houses, you know, all were derelict houses, but there wasn't enough to go round. So they would let so many sleep in a room and things like that. So many slept in over-crowded rooms and were glad to get them."

The initial experience of a few ex-servicemen, such as Stanley Hodges, Gerry Smith and Robert Murray, were not in keeping with the fate suffered by others. Stanley Hodges asserts that he once resided in a house with a family and two other black people. He elaborates:

> "This particular landlady, we found, was very understanding towards us, very kind, and her family at the time consisted of three sons. We all seemed to be part of that particular family and we were well accepted, well treated, and this was one of the moments I cherish and never will forget."

Gerry Smith also recalls an episode which reveals the supportive and caring nature of some people, in particular white women. He gives

155

the example of deciding to leave the job he had in West Croydon after being refused a promotion because of his colour. But then he faced the dual problem of finding employment and accommodation:

"I met a lady on the bus coming home from work one evening. We got talking and I told her my problem. The lady, who agreed with me, worked at the Colonial Office. She said, 'Don't let me down but I am going to give you the name of someone who could help you to get another job.' As a result of her recommendation I got a job with a well-known firm in Derby and worked there for almost thirty-two years, up to my retirement."

However, for Gerry and many others at the time, procuring suitable places to live in posed a definite problem, barring a few exceptions which could never be forgotten. Gerry Smith, after being regularly refused accommodation, recollects:

"Then a Scottish lady said she would take me and my friend in. This was in Derby. The irony of it was that she had a party to which some of the same friends who objected to us as lodgers were invited. She had a small organ and I was the only one who could play it. They were most impressed and when she told them what model boarders we were, they were all anxious to house us saying that if she was ever on holiday they would put us up."

Describing an affable encounter, one ex-serviceman states that when he was a student he procured lodgings with full board quite easily:

"From the time I appeared at the door in one of the most fashionable streets, I was welcomed with open arms by the landlady. She was a most pleasant old lady with a benign smile, being extremely obliging and attentive to my needs for a long time."

However this serene existence was to change when he announced to her one night that he was getting married. It was as though he had done her the gravest injury. Her genuine smile vanished immediately and she blinked, appearing to be deep in thought. He goes on to say:

"Those words triggered off alarm bells in her mind. You could see her brain working overtime.
    'Married!' she gasped, as though it had taken her unaware. She

156

seemed lost for words, removing her glasses. I could sense the inevitable question lurking in the background.

'Who is she?' she asked.

'A woman' I said facetiously.

'I know that! What is she?.... I mean is she one of your own people?' I knew what she was getting at, but I just carried on my tomfoolery!!"

His wife duly moved in with him and for a short time they were alright until the birth of their first child, which complicated the situation and resulted in a gradual deterioration in the relationship, and finally he and his family were given their notice to leave.

So, once again, as with their experience of gaining employment, the Westindian ex-servicemen had to rely on the good-hearted nature of individuals when it came to finding lodgings. For instance, Pasteur Irons, who was well paid when working down the coal mines, bought a house and gave lodgings to two ex-servicemen who lived locally. Stanley Hodges also recalls the friendliness and kindness that resulted in his acquiring lodgings. In his case, while he lived in Nottingham, an elderly man offered him lodgings:

"One particular person I have in mind was an old gentleman who one day came up to me and said, ' Stan, where are you living?' and I told him 'I'm living at the hostel, not far away.' He said, 'Would you like to come and live with us?' I said, 'Yes please' because obviously life in the hostel was not an ideal situation so I was very glad indeed of this offer. I went to lodge with him and his wife in Heanor."

As in the workplace, the Westindian ex-servicemen were at the mercy, usually, of a landlady. The fickleness of these landladies would leave the Westindian ex-servicemen homeless without any means of redress. While in Birmingham George Powe recalls an incident that reveals the powerlessness that afflicted them:

".... this lady decided to give us bed spaces. We were given a room and I think there were four of us in the room .... However ..... we were there only for a week and the woman decided to chase us out because she claimed that one of the lads made eyes at her daughter. So she chased us out of the house and so we went out not having anywhere to live."

In an attempt to obtain lodgings, and other necessities, Westindians would form cartels. These cartels were called 'partners' and are still practised by some Westindians today. What this cartel essentially entailed was for a group of individuals to pool a set sum of their weekly wage together and give it to one of the individuals in the cartel one week for them to use as they wished. The following week another individual was given the money and so it would continue until each and every person in the 'partner' had received a 'hand'. After every one had received a 'hand' of the 'partner', people could re-negotiate as to whether to continue in the 'partner' or cease participating.

Even with money, Westindian people had difficulties, as George Powe claims:

> "At that time a few black people tried to buy houses and were not able to. One or two wanted to buy cars and they had difficulties. You would be surprised that they had difficulties in buying cars. Those who managed to buy cars could not get insurances and this happened in Nottingham."

According to Athleston Holder, the greatest racism that the ex-servicemen were to face, especially non-white ex-servicemen, occurred outside of the workplace. He claims that he only met minor incidents through discrimination. Here he recalls one incident when he was pursued by a policeman:

> "I remember going to work one morning, in the early 1960s, catching a bus in Victoria Street, Derby. I felt a hand in my back and a man, who described himself as a detective, said to me, 'You look like a man wanted for murder in Birmingham.' I replied, 'What has that got to do with me?' That man pursued me for a long time until I went to see the superintendent of police and told him in no uncertain terms to get that officer off my back. That was the last I heard from that officer."

Those individuals whose partners were not black were obvious targets for comments. An ex-serviceman who had married an Irish woman and, as a result, was to have remarks directed his way, comments:

> "People used to make jokes about cotton and shillelagh, you know what that signifies? Cotton for the blacks and shillelagh for the Irish. This

158

didn't mean much to me at the time."

Nevertheless, prejudice and race bigotry were not monopolised by white people alone. Black people, too, looked upon inter-race relationships with great disfavour and could be most venomous in their disapproval. The same ex-serviceman remembers being specially warned by his father on his departure to Britain:

> "... 'And don't bring no white woman back here.' Now I had gone and allied myself in exactly that manner."

He goes on to state:

> "True, I was a grown man and I was thousands of miles away. True, there weren't any black women around at the time, and the Bible does say 'It's better to marry than to burn!' but I can hear my father saying 'Shut up Boy-man! You disobeyed me!!'"

He was to agonize for months as to the best way to break the news to his father. Then he came up with a "most inspired idea": to tell his father that he had got married to a beautiful coloured Irish woman. His father's reply was swift to arrive:

> "I know we're supposed to live in the jungle out here, but I've never heard of a bloody black Irish anybody before! Well caught sir!"

The truth was unravelled without any help from the deceiver.

Pasteur Irons had also married a white woman and recalls people staring as he and his wife walked down the streets and goes on to tell about the racism he faced:

> "People stared at us all the time. Even when we stared back, they couldn't take their eyes off us, and I suffered many more indignities unknown to my wife. Some I forgot about but others remain with me. It was embarrassing for me to tell my wife, you know, how I was treated so badly. Even to this day I haven't told my wife how badly we were being treated."

In fact, such was the extent of the hostility that was directed towards him that he would predominantly shop at Woolworth's because it was a self-service shop. In one instance, he went to a church and was told by the Priest that he would rather if black people, who "love church," did not attend his church. On another occasion he protested about the treatment he encountered on a bus:

> "I purchased a 4p ticket. The conductor clipped the ticket and threw it on the floor. I asked him why he did that, he said I could pick it up. I reported him to the first bus-inspector I saw. The conductor was told in no uncertain way that he was wrong, and to make sure that on further occasions that the ticket was placed in my hand."

While the denial of jobs and accommodation represented the worst examples of the prejudices that Westindians encountered, there was no shortage of other forms of discrimination and prejudices, such as racist comments being made in the earshot of individuals, being addressed in a derogatory manner and off-handed treatment. One incident recalled by an ex-air serviceman occurred at Euston Railway station, London, when he asked a porter the directions to the "urinal":

> "You who?', the porter erupted.
> 'The urinal,' the ex-serviceman repeated, indicating.
> 'Ooooh, you mean the gents!' the porter finally realised.
> As I walked away to the toilets I overheard the porter saying: 'These bloody people from the jungle don't even know what the gents is!"

Yet another ex-serviceman encountered a very embarrassing and degrading experience in a pub. He recalls the day, a very hot summer's day, when, after a game of cricket, he could have "murdered a pint." He walked into a pub that was full and bided his time while people all around him were being served, some more than once. Many came in after him and had their fill while he stood patiently. He finally ventured to give his order only to be refused point blank. He would never forget his personal feelings at the time:

> "I had to take myself, my little case containing my cricket kit, my unquenched thirst and walk slowly home. On my way home turmoil was raging in my head. I was taking stock of myself and, for the first time in my life, I was asking myself: Why have I travelled thousands of miles to be on the receiving end of such treatment? I was as British, nay, I considered myself more British than the British .... and more patriotic

than the most fanatic Anglophile! Why should a man be penalized for offering his services?"

This incident was to wound his pride deeply, resulting in his walking home in floods of tears. As he continued to analyse this experience and philosophise about his life, the seeds of doubt were beginning to be sown in his mind:

"Can you imagine how I must have felt as I walked along with my case in hand? All manner of thoughts came to my mind. My tiny island of Jamaica, barely 4,000 square miles in area, had been loyal enough to present the Mother Country - Britain - with a squadron of Spitfires at the beginning of the War. I had no idea how much that amounted to in terms of money, but I couldn't help feeling that if that sum, whatever it was, had been used to keep people like me at home instead of exposing us to this humiliation, it would have been far better spent."

In some cases, this racism was to cause brawls of the type that the Westindian servicemen had become well accustomed to during the War years. George Powe's explanation for these pugilistic encounters was "sheer naked racism":

"White people generally were hostile to blacks because they said we were lowering the standard of this country. We were given the menial jobs because, even then just after the War, a lot of white men wouldn't take the jobs that Westindians were given, so they were hostile to us because of that. The other thing was that the black ex-servicemen were very young and as with, you know, youthfulness, you tended to show off, and used to dress up and go to dances, mess around with girls. They felt that you were taking away the girls, and the girls shouldn't associate with blacks."

Pasteur Irons also recalls fights happening in Long Eaton where he lived and the response from the police force:

"Fighting developed and the police came and they said all Westindians were barred from Long Eaton town itself. Yes! We couldn't go in the town ..... and I only lived a mile away. Then what they tried to do in the pubs and all that, they refused to serve us, but I got to know one or two of the landlords .... We didn't take any notice."

161

Gerald Beard sums up the conflict as being based on the general attitudes of white men:

> "Well the thing that I can say is that they were rather selfish, particularly the white men, who liked everything for themselves and you should go without. That's how I found them, really."

One salient incident that, for Pasteur Irons, embodied the isolation and disrespect that Westindian people suffered was the response and help he gained when his wife became ill:

> " My wife had a nervous breakdown and she had to go in to hospital. I was brought up a Roman Catholic all my life ...... I had three young children aged three, two, and one, you know ..... I had to look after them. I couldn't go to work so I went to the Catholic Church. They didn't want to know ..... (I) tried (the) Salvation Army, (they sent me to see a Sister Teresa) .... so I went and the Sister, who said, 'What can you afford to pay to look after three children?' I said 'I don't know', so she phoned social services and they said they would help me. They said it was £3 each per week and in those days my wages were only about £6. It was £3 each a week which was £9 .... social services took them and they said I have to pay half, so I was paying half out of my earnings - and my wife was still in hospital. I didn't come and see them for the first fortnight. So when I went back after the fortnight I never knew humans could be treated like that. My children looked like inmates of Belsen concentration camp. Their hair wasn't combed, they had lice in their hair, their shoes were worn out, they had odd clothes on, oh! I have never seen such a sight in my life. I nearly had a nervous breakdown myself."

As a result of the racism, hostility and ignorance that Westindians encountered some of the ex-servicemen formed social clubs or became politically active. Pasteur Irons, George Powe and Stanley Hodges were three individuals, who became actively involved in trying to change the situation they saw black individuals encountering. Pasteur Irons, with twelve other people, formed a group which was concerned with issues like housing and welfare. As he states, this group was very powerless:

> "We couldn't use anything else but negotiation because, with just a dozen of us, we couldn't do anything else. We had no means, just word of mouth, you know, just sitting around the table, trying to persuade,

that's all we could do. We felt violence wouldn't get us anywhere so we used persuasion and we spoke to anyone who would listen."

George Powe's interest in political issues was stimulated by the political culture that existed in Liverpool and seeing black people enduring a similar plight in Birmingham as in Liverpool. On his political perspective he asserts:

"Well, I was Left Wing. At the time I was not a member of the Communist Party yet; it was when I came to Nottingham that I joined the Communist Party. Although I moved around the Communist Party for a long time, I was never fully-fledged ...... to fight some of the abuses that were meted out to us, for example, the abuse when we went for jobs. We were also fighting for homes in Birmingham."

Stanley Hodges set up a social club as he describes:

"I think in 1951, a group of ex-servicemen formed the Westindian Caribbean Cricket Club in Derby, Nottingham, and the immediate area. We didn't set out to build a separate community but we realized that at least getting together would provide us with an outlet socially, and of course it naturally took us more into the community as such."

Together with others he had set up the first black social organization in the country which is still in existence today under the name of Westindian National Association, ACNA. He describes the original purpose of this organization:

"We didn't involve ourselves in the direct political issues, as such. We were still doing or contributing, in our way, towards easing the tension that there was. We realized when we went out to play cricket it was mainly against the local white population and wherever we went we were well accepted, well respected well treated, and weren't being patronized. We wouldn't tolerate that. We tried to conduct ourselves to show respect and expected to be shown respect. I think we have done that, so I think on a whole we thought we weren't politically motivated, we were doing what we thought was our thing in our own way to ease the situation."

In considering the progress black people have made in Britain, Gerald Beard's views are optimistic:

"Today as I go around to many of these offices in town I see coloured people holding, more or less, what I would call vital positions. In those days you didn't see that. In that case I think things have improved."

James Moore's daughter also echoes this tone of optimism:

"The strange thing about it, those neighbours we used to fall out with because we were black are the same people today, surprisingly enough, who are either married to blacks or have got black children, or they are right in the black community now."

Dickens wrote: "it was the best of times, it was the worst of times"- such was the experience for those who left sun-blessed islands in the Caribbean. James Mckenzie, Norma Best and Gerald Beard voice their reflections on life in Britain which are worth noting. James Mckenzie claims:

"I've lived a very happy family life until illness conquered me and I decided to return to the land of my birth. I would like to think of England as my second home. If I should live my life again I would do it all over again."

Norma Best affirms:

"I've enjoyed every moment of it."

Gerald Beard takes a more philosophical perspective of his experience in Britain when he reflects on whether he had a reasonably good life in England, better than he might have lived if he stopped in the Caribbean. He states:

".... when I went home I saw many there who have done so well for themselves that I thought to myself, 'Well, I should have stopped there.' The trouble is, when you come here and fight for the white people and then they turn and fight you, it leaves a nasty taste in your mouth. According to them, you have done nothing - they don't want you to equal them at all in any respect. Finding it like that, I think, is my main reason why I said that if I knew what things would be like here, I would not have come back. But I think to myself, 'Well, there's no sense in thinking about it now because spilt milk is something that cannot be replaced. What is done is done!"

164

THE JAMAICA INTERVIEWS: THOSE WHO DID NOT RETURN TO THE UK

Broadly speaking, those Westindians - whether RAF groundcrew or aircrew - who contributed towards World War II in the UK - fell into three groups as to what they did when the War ended.

Firstly, there were those who returned to their native islands or countries immediately after the termination of hostilities, some returning to the UK shortly afterwards, others finding their way back over a period of years.

Secondly, those who, having served in the UK during the War, never returned to their homelands when it finished, electing instead to stay in Britain.

Thirdly, those who found their own countries more alluring, preferring to remain. This chapter is concerned with this third group - those who never returned to the UK.

There are many men and women who did their bit in the UK towards the War effort and about whom nothing more has ever been heard. No doubt, some of these contributors are still active and are probably preserving the memory of the RAF through associations in their own home branches - in Guyana (then British Guiana), Belize (then British Honduras), Trinidad and Tobago, Barbados, The Leeward & Windward Islands, the Bahamas, Bermuda and, of course, Jamaica.

Ulric Cross of Trinidad has previously been mentioned as one who never returned to the UK to live permanently. Neither did Arthur Wint, who became a Flight Lieutenant and who qualified as a doctor after the War, except returning as Jamaica High Commissioner. However, there are many others, far too numerous to mention here, but certainly ample evidence abounds in Jamaica to show that this is so. The person largely responsible for highlighting their activities was one Vincent Miller, now deceased, who went to Jamaica at his own expense in 1984 and devoted the greater part of his holidays there to recording the voices of some of those ex-RAF personnel who never returned to the UK - ex-servicemen like Alfred Keith Levy, Dudley Thompson, Oliver Marshall, Ralph Walker, Del Frank Smith to mention but a few.

Vin also obtained details of the formation and progress of the Jamaica Branch of the RAF Association. These recordings have since become known as the JAMAICA INTERVIEWS. Vin Miller was a man of great character, dedication, courage and singularity of purpose. Above all he held the Nottingham WI Ex-Services Association in the highest regards, doing everything in his power to project its image.

The Jamaica Branch of the RAF Association was established in August 1946. This is quite amazing in view of the fact that the War only ended one year earlier. One doubts whether many other RAF Associations in other parts of the world were started more speedily after the cessation of hostilities. Their official motto is **Non Novis Said Ovis**, meaning Not For Ourselves Alone, which they have tried to live up to over the many years since their formation under their founder President, Dudley Thompson. Another of their laudable ideals is never to mention rank at meetings - ABANDON RANK ALL THOSE THAT ENTER HERE is their permanent resolution.

From August 1946, the Jamaica Branch of the RAF Association has never looked back and has gone from strength to strength. They have done many things, including building their own headquarters along with the Jamaica Legion in December 1961 just in time for their very first independence celebrations in 1962. Since then the HQ has been extremely useful in entertaining all the visiting service personnel - the Army, the Navy and the Air Force from all over the world. Among their other achievements are fighting for their own welfare, facilities of the Arthur Meeney ex-RAF personnel, helping to maintain the ex-services club, and, this is their greatest pride and joy, donating the very first 'Home' in the Cheshire Homes Village in 1975.

The Cheshire Homes Village idea was the brain-child of the late Group Captain Leonard Cheshire VC, one of the most highly-decorated British airmen of World War II, renowned for being a prolific air-destroyer of Germany. At the end of the War he was invited to observe the dropping of the atomic bomb over Nagasaki, Japan and, as a result of this horrific experience, his outlook on life was completely changed to such an extent that he resolved to devote the rest of his life towards helping the disabled. So, together with his wife, he set up the first home for the disabled, named after himself - The Cheshire Homes.

The idea grew and houses in model Cheshire Villages in some forty-eight countries throughout the world have now been established, including Jamaica, some of whose ex-RAF personnel had the honour and pleasure of meeting the Group Captain. The interviews were held at the Headquarters of the Jamaica RAF Association, Curphey Place, Kingston, and was a very prestigious occasion. All of those mentioned have been officers of the Association over the years. Alfred Keith Levy was a past Vice-President and Manager of the Jamaica ex-services Club. After learning of the success of certain individuals in England, he says:

> "Perhaps it might have been better for me to have stayed there but, nevertheless, the progress that we have made in Jamaica is really amazing, causing most of us that stayed behind not to regret it."

Oliver Marshall was Chairman of the Association for 17 years and President for nine years in succession to Del Frank Smith. At the time of Vin Miller's visit both Dudley Thompson and Del Frank Smith were honouring as Vice-Presidents. It was Oliver Marshall that gave a brief resume of the history of the Jamaica RAF Association.

Many Westindians joining the RAF aircrew received their initial training in Canada, a large number passing out as officers. After this training they were flown to England. Dudley Thompson, a Flight Lieutenant, recalls his parents, like those of many of the other boys, expressing the usual concern that he was going far away from home but this deterred neither him nor, indeed, any of the others. So, he found himself in England, among many peoples, for the first time seeing the City of London that he had often heard of and read about, viewing the usual sights - Buckingham Palace, Nelson's Column, the Houses of Parliament, Whitehall, Numbers 10 and 11 Downing Street, Big Ben and many more for the first time.

"So this is the Motherland," he sighed to himself. It was, for him, not just a challenge but a bit of a thrill sharing in the hustle and bustle of the capital with its different peoples - the Indian with his turban, the African in his flowing garments, Poles, Americans and the miscellany of languages that assailed the ear. His friends were all Westindians.

> "But whether you were Guyanese, Barbadians, Trinidadians, Jamaicans, English, Australian or New Zealander, you were all one; there was no doubt that you were going to answer any call that came. I had no preconceptions of the country. I knew they had good universities, a very advanced civilization and that it was a developed country. I knew she did not have our sunshine, our sugar and fruits - that they sent people to our countries who did a lot for us - like our school masters, like my own headmaster - a Mr. Newman who was a Flight Captain. I had no concerns about being a black Jamaican in England. None whatsoever. I had no experience of anything like prejudice."

The first stark reality of the War, as Dudley remembers, was not in terms of shooting or bombing, but when the train stopped at one railway station and they saw ice-cream:

> "The boys were excited! But the ice-cream, believe it or not, tasted to them like something made without sugar. Why make ice-cream without sugar? We couldn't understand it until we began to realize that we were in a different world - a country at War - everything, including sugar, was in short supply - rationed!"

They found it difficult accustoming themselves to the food, sometimes resorting to eating dried fruit. Coming from the Caribbean, one did not find it easy to adjust to the new cuisine. Throughout all the stages of recruitment, they were told that the requirements for the RAF were very strict. Before the War, standards, particularly amongst the aircrew, were quite high, and the aim during the War, even with substantially increased numbers, was to preserve these standards. However, the boys encountered no problems so far as standards were concerned. It just took a bit of time to get into the marching. Dudley remembers doing operational training and going to Heaton Park, Manchester, then finding himself in Brighton, though he is hazy about the reason for being there. The part of his training he remembers most is his stay at Cranwell, the RAF College in Lincolnshire. He first started on single engines and afterwards they put him on Oxfords for some time. He says:

168

"At training I was just a member of the crew. I knew we lost a gunner, Martin, whose mother was an oldish Scottish woman. She was an extremely nice old lady who respected black people. She really welcomed me."

England struck him as being a far more beautiful country, even in war-time, than he had imagined. He pictured each Englishman having a little garden in his back yard and looking after it.

"They did impress one with their love for the square garden plot. Most of them worked in the mines, going underground every morning."

To him:

"It was an unforgettable picture of courage and guts of a people without the slightest thought of giving up, having no fear whatsoever, knowing that in the end, all was going to come alright."

And yet, in all the operations he carried out, he never fought with any other Westindian as a member of his crew. There happened to be one or two other Westindians at the same station, sometimes in the same squadron, but he moved from squadron to squadron according to requirements and was not in any one place for any length of time. He continues:

"I left flying actually as a Flight Lieutenant and was sent to do lots of special jobs. I would say that colour or race never in any way affected the relations. Never at any time did I see any situation of colour friction between members of crew."

After flying, he was seconded to the Colonial Office as an officer. There he met an old friend, Jamaican Flying Officer Ruby. They worked together for a long time. Both studied Law, although Dudley qualified first. Dudley was then sent to Jamaica escorting returning Westindians to their homelands. He was accompanied by Officer Bunting who was a Flight Commander at the time.

On his return to England, he went back to the Colonial Office when he made visits to most of the stations with Westindian servicemen. He saw them, listened to what they had to say and tried

169

to communicate with them. He needed some ideas and advice about what should happen regarding their resettlement.

> "I really thought the RAF and the RAF Association had been a good discipline to all of us."

At the luncheon at the RAF Association Headquarters in Jamaica, ex-servicemen were unanimous in their confirmation of being proud to fight for the Mother Country, each re-affirming that he would do the same again if circumstances were repeated. They also took pride in the fact that they, as indeed everyone else - aircrew or groundcrew - were all volunteers.

> "It is for this reason that they viewed with some considerable pain problems that have since arisen in the UK - with regards to colour."

This was to do, in particular, with the Immigration Laws. Strong feelings were expressed that, as an act of recognition, "any ex-serviceman who actually served in the United Kingdom during the War should be accorded the same rights as Patrials, and that the Jamaica RAF Association should pass a resolution to that effect." It was, however, concluded that any such initiative should come from the UK Parliament as it was their Law - under their jurisdiction.

Vin Miller gave his thanks on behalf of the Nottingham Westindian Ex-Services Association and promised on his return to speak to those who could make representations. He wished that some of his colleagues back in England were present to experience what he had experienced on that day. It was something he would treasure for the rest of his life. Unfortunately, he passed away before he could execute his promise.

A HISTORY OF No. 139
(JAMAICA) SQUADRON, RAF

Not entirely divorced from the previous chapter is the history of No. 139 (Jamaica) Squadron - Royal Air Force by Oliver Marshall, past Chairman and President of the Royal Air Force Association (Jamaica) who, at the time of writing the brief history, was its sole surviving Honorary Member. So relevant is this history that no account of Westindian involvement in the World Wars - both I and II - would be complete without some reference being made to the Squadron. No 139 Squadron of the Royal Air Force - wrote Marshall - was originally formed and equipped with Bristol Fighters in Italy towards the end of World War I in July 1918, but did not have the name of Jamaica attached to it until early in World War II. In 1940 the late Mr Alec Gordon OBE, JP Planter and Penkeeper of Darx Hall estate at the time and more recently of Bonham Spring both in the Parish of St Ann's, Jamaica, heard the following appeal broadcast in a speech by the late Sir Winston Churchill, famous wartime Prime Minister of Great Britain:

> "Is not this the appointed time for all to make the utmost exertions in their power? If the battle is to be won we must provide our men with ever-increasing quantities of the weapons and ammunition they need. We must have, and have quickly, more aeroplanes, more tanks, more shells, more guns."

As a result of this Mr Gordon was so inspired that he immediately started the Jamaica Bombing Plane Fund, with the ready assistance and co-operation of Jamaica's *Daily Gleaner*. This fund, subsequently described as the Bombers for Britain Fund, caught on like wildfire throughout the Commonwealth realizing eventually many millions of pounds.

Under the management of the late Mr Michael deCordova, the *Gleaner* within ten days collected £20,000 with the response from every section of the Jamaica community being most enthusiastic and generous. The firms of Henriques Bros., Henderson Bros., and Fred L

171

Myers & Son each donated one bomber, and finally Jamaica's contribution was enough to provide an entire Squadron of twelve Bristol Blenheim medium bombers. This achievement by the people of Jamaica caused Sir Winston Churchill to be so impressed and grateful that in appreciation No 139 Squadron was renamed the 139 (Jamaica) Squadron in April 1941 and he decreed that the Island of Jamaica should have a squadron of the Royal Air Force named after it "so long as there will be a Royal Air Force."

In commemoration of the Island's mighty effort Lord Beaverbrook (then Britain's Minister of Aircraft Production) presented to the *Daily Gleaner* a plaque with the following inscription:

> "IN THE HOUR OF PERIL THE PEOPLE OF JAMAICA (through the *Jamaica Gleaner*) EARNED THE GRATITUDE OF THE BRITISH NATIONS, SUSTAINING THE VALOUR OF THE ROYAL AIR FORCE AND FORTIFYING THE CAUSE OF FREEDOM BY THE GIFT OF BOMBER AIRCRAFT.
> "They shall mount up with wings as eagles."

Subsequently Mr Alex Gordon was awarded the OBE for his part in pioneering this tremendous accomplishment.

The 139 (Jamaica) Squadron has a very distinguished record of service both in war and peace. Within an hour after war was declared on September 3rd 1939, a Blenheim of the Squadron took off to reconnoitre German naval bases, the pilot of the aircraft Flying Officer A McPherson being the first officer to be awarded the Distinguished Flying Cross in World War II; and very near to VE day in May 1945, Mosquitos from the Squadron were part of a Bomber Command Force which attacked Kiel. Thus the Squadron enjoyed the unique achievement of having taken part in the first and last RAF operational sorties of World War II. The Squadron has been disbanded and reformed several times. First disbanded in 1919 at the end of the Great War, it was reformed with Hawker Hinds in 1936 and at the outbreak of World War II was equipped with Blenheims. It was again temporarily disbanded in 1942 but in September of that year was once again reformed and made fully operational with the famous DeHaviland Mosquito. In 1943 the Squadron joined the renowned Pathfinder Force of Bombers Command which it served in

8 Group until the end of the war.

Based first at Wyton then at Upwood in Huntingdonshire, it attained a high reputation for accuracy of navigation and bombing and was noted for its precision operations, among its most outstanding being participation in raids on the Gestapo Headquarters in Oslo, the bombing of the molybdenum plant at Knaben in Norway and the bombing of a diesel works in Copenhagen. It also took part in the first daylight operation on Berlin, which was effective enough to cause Goering, who was broadcasting an important speech at the time, to go off the air! During World War II the Jamaica Squadron flew more than 4,000 operational sorties, dropped more than 1,500 tons of bombs and had more than 150 of its members decorated. Surprisingly, few Jamaicans served with the Squadron but among those who did, the following are personally known to the writer: the late Flt/Lt Harold Coke-Kerr, DFC (who won his decoration while serving with the Squadron and died after the War), Flt/Lt John Ebanks, DFM (a Vice-President of the Jamaica Branch of RAFA) and Messrs Vernon Mendes and Douglas Roberts (both members of RAFA Jamaica). At their base at Wittering near Peterborough, several Jamaicans were serving with the groundcrew of the Squadron, which was then equipped with Handley Page Victor MK IIB pure jet V-bombers armed with Blue Steel stand-off nuclear missile as a part of the Britain's contribution to NATO Western deterrent.

The Squadron's motto is *Si Placet Necamus* - We Destroy at Will - and reference to its Battle Honours bears ample testimony to the truth of this boast.

Up to the time of writing, the Squadron has paid four visits altogether to Jamaica, with a fifth confidently expected to take place soon. The first visit was in August, 1955 when as a feature attraction of "Jamaica 300" (the Island's Tercentenary Celebrations of membership in the British family of nations), the then Governor of Jamaica Sir Hugh Foot - later Lord Caradon, Britain's Permanent Representative to the United Nations - was instrumental in having them spend five days here.

The force was comprised of eight English Electric Canberra B6 pure jet medium bombers from their base in Binbrook in Lincolnshire with three ground support Hastings of Transport Command. The

Force Commander was Air Vice-Marshal J R Whitely AOC 3 Group who became Air Marshal Sir John Whitley KBE, CB, DSO, AFA, RAF (Retd) and Controller of the RAF Benevolent Fund. This long-standing association with Sir John Whitley is of particular interest to Jamaica as the RAF Benevolent Fund spends large sums of money annually to relieve distress and hardship among ex-RAF personnel on the Island. This assistance is administered by the Jamaica Committee of the Fund, which is a compliment to Jamaica, as it is the only country outside the United Kingdom which has its own local Committee of the Fund. This is in deference to the large number of Jamaicans who saw voluntary service in the RAF during World War II.

The Squadron Commander at the time of the first visit was Sqd/Ldr Arthur (Artie) Ashworth, DSO, DFC & Bar, AFC, of 'walrus moustache' fame, and during this first visit the Freedom of the City of Kingston was bestowed upon the members of the Squadron at a very impressive Civic Ceremony in the George VI Park. They were special guests at a glittering Ball held in honour by the Jamaica Branch of RAFA at the Royal Jamaica Yacht Club, Alec Gordon entertained them in St Ann, and they thrilled the entire Island with their daring flying displays.

Their next visit was in August 1962 when they were invited by the Jamaica Government to take part in the Island's Independence celebrations. On this occasion four Victor MK1 bombers from their base in Wittering and one ground support Britannia made up the force which was commanded by Air Vice-Marshal Brian Burnet AOC 3 Group at Mildenhall, who as Air Chief Marshal Sir Brian Burnett, KCB, DFC, became one of the leading officers of the entire RAF. The Squadron was commanded by Wing Commander Brian Plenderleith, and again the Government and RAFA arranged a series of enjoyable functions to entertain them and they gave several impressive flying displays over Kingston and around the Island. In August 1966 much to our delight they again spent the best part of a week with us, this time invited by our Government for the Commonwealth Games. Three Victor MK.IIB bombers and one Britannia comprised the force which was under the command of Air Vice-Marshal Denis Smallwood, CB, CBE, DSO, DFC, AOC 3 Group at Mildenhall, and the Squadron was commanded by Wing Commander Douglas Bell, DFC, AFC. Very sadly, only a month before the arrival of the

174

Squadron, Mr Alec Gordon died quite suddenly at the grand old age of 86 and was buried at Bonham Spring on July 2nd. He had been eagerly looking forward to their visit and had joined in the planning of it during the June visit of the 3 Group HQ Operations Officer and Deputy Force Commander, Wing Commander John Beddoes, himself a former CO of the Squadron during the period of Sir Donald Sangster's first visit to them in 1965. Members of the Squadron made a special pilgrimage to his grave where Wing Commander Bell laid a wreath and at that precise moment, as a tribute to the esteem and affection in which Alec Gordon was held by 'his' Jamaica Squadron, a Victor flew over Bonham Spring trailing the Jamaica colours in smoke from its exhaust. As founder of the Squadron Alec Gordon had been its only Honorary Member throughout the years, and during a RAFA party to welcome them at Curphey Place this particular honour was transferred to the Chairman of the Jamaica Branch of RAFA, of which the writer, as incumbent, is immensely proud. RAFAs return gesture was to make the current and every future Commanding Officer of the Jamaica Squadron an Honorary Vice-President of Our Jamaica Branch. It was also during this visit that the Squadron presented the magnificent Jamaica Squadron Trophy to the Government's Youth Development Agency of the Ministry of Youth and Community Development for perpetual annual football competition among the Youth Clubs of Jamaica. The presentation took place at a most delightful reception in the Squadron's honour held at Vale Royal by the then Acting Prime Minister of Jamaica, the late Sir Donald Sangster KCVO who was a great admirer and favourite of the Squadron, having visited them at Wittering on at least two occasions.

Their latest visit took place during Battle of Britain Week in September 1967 and was made by one Victor MK.IIB bomber which, through the good offices of the British High Commissioner in Jamaica, came specially all the way as a splendid gesture to celebrate with RAFA Jamaica the 21st Anniversary of their Branch. The aircraft was captained by Group Captain Paul Malloire, AFC, Officer Commanding RAF Station Wittering (himself a former CO of the Squadron during one of Alec Gordon's visits to them), and the Squadron Commander, Wing Commander Douglas Bell, was his co-pilot. Their five days spent in Jamaica as very welcome personal guests of RAFA members, developed into one long happy birthday party!

The Squadron has always had a warm and very hospitable welcome for any Jamaican visitors who find their way to its base in Britain, and over the years many Jamaicans and representatives of Jamaica have proved this to be true, among them being Mr Alec Gordon, Sir Hugh Foot and Sir Kenneth Blackburne (former Governors of Jamaica), Sir Donald Sangster, HE Sir Laurence Lindo (Jamaica High Commissioner to Britain), Mr Aston Foreman (Deputy High Commissioner), Senator Hector Wynter, Brigadier David Smith (Chief of Staff, Jamaica Defence Force), Mr Gordon Langdon (Commissioner of Police), Colonels Mascoll, Robinson, Moody, and the writer and his wife.

Together with several other Jamaicans, the writer was privileged to pay a particularly memorable visit to the Squadron at Wittering in June 1967 when specially invited to the Presentation of their Standard by HRH Princess Margaret, which took place at a most impressive and colourful Ceremonial Parade in typically Jamaican weather! It was declared certainly one of the finest hours in the Squadron's history and was declared an outstanding success from every angle. One couldn't help noticing with a feeling of sentimental satisfaction the presence of several Jamaica airmen in the Guard of Honour and elsewhere on the parade ground, and also one had been specially chosen to drive Princess Margaret's car. Among many other items on the day's programme were most interesting and historic Static and Flying Displays which included a Bristol Fighter of Squadron service in 1918, a Hawker Hind of 1936, a Mosquito of 1943-5, a Canberra of 1955 and of course a Victor of 1967; and also an incredibly spectacular 'Scramble' and take-off demonstration by four Victors in the record time of well under two minutes.

Over many years strong, active and affectionate ties have existed between the Squadron and Jamaica, and it was heart-warming as a Jamaican to see the Jamaican flag flying proudly at their Headquarters and to see their aircrews wearing scarves made in our National colours as a part of their standard flying kit, both at home and abroad. Every Christmas, gifts of rum, cigars and fruit are sent by the government and people of Jamaica to the Squadron, and during all their visits to our country appropriate gifts have been exchanged between the Squadron and RAFA and more recently the JDF as well.

A very warm Jamaica welcome is extended to the new CO of 'our' Squadron Wing Commander Frank McClory, who succeeded Wing Commander Bell at the end of last year, and it is our earnest hope that long may this glorious and historic Inter-Commonwealth link last!

CONCLUSION

Watching the dusted-off cans of archive films used periodically for documentaries and the War films of Ealing and Rank studios; seeing the black and white photographs of uniformed men and women linked arm in arm; reading the countless books of the heroic deeds individuals performed in defeating The Third Reich, one would quite rightly believe that the Second World War was exclusively fought by British white individuals. However, these portrayals often tend to disregard the substantial contributions - military and otherwise made by men and women of the Indian and African Continents, those from the Near, Middle and Far East and, of course, those from the Caribbean, Central and South America.

The passage of time has obviously caused some experiences to slip into the sub-conscious of the ex-service personnel, resulting in some participants contributing more than others. But this should not detract from the collective nature of the experiences articulated, for, as detailed, a great deal of similarities exist in some of the accounts given. Hence the preponderance of one person's account over another should be seen as embroidering the experiences that all may have had to varying degrees. That is, adding fine detail to common themes of experiences encountered by the Westindian war veterans.

From the accounts given in this book one immediately senses the esteem, kinship and deep-rooted attachment with which the service personnel construed Britain. Fashioned by a history of economic, social and political links, a romanticized image of Britain was forged in the consciousness of the Westindians. For these individuals, whilst in the Caribbean, being a colonized people was not seen in an oppressive, dehumanizing light. To be one of 'His Majesty's' subjects was to be held in high regards, not too surprisingly after black people had been fleeced of their heritage and assimilated into a Eurocentric life-style. So ingrained was the affinity to Britain, and such was the deification heaped on her by the colonies themselves, that Barbados was proud to view itself as a miniature imitation of England, with England being viewed as a colossus from which it was cloned.

This feeling of inter-dependence galvanized individuals from the various Islands within the Caribbean to enlist into the British Armed Forces as well as to volunteer to work in factories which contributed to the war effort. These individuals participated in a number of activities and hailed from a variety of backgrounds. Remembering that most of the recruits were in their teens, with all the youthful exuberance usually present in this period of young lives, ideas of fairness and an equal opportunity to fulfil ambitions were vibrant in the recruits' minds, as typified by Dudley Thompson's comment of, "the spirit of the RAF." Such reflections encapsulated the view then held of Britain. Moreover, as an ex-serviceman alludes, the circumstances that existed at the time offered further powerful motivating force for individuals to strive to get over to Britain to widen horizons, to seek adventure and to encourage the prospect of limitless opportunities.

All these features conspired to mould the Westindian service personnel's conception of Britain as being their motherland and a land of untold opportunity. Aroused within the Westindian service personnel was an expectation that Britain would welcome its sons and daughters with open arms. So Vera Lynn's war-time lullaby, beckoning the 'blue bird over the white cliffs of Dover,' was whole-heartedly harmonized in a chorus of British pride and defiance by the Westindian service personnel. However, unlike the lost family member who returned from the wilderness and received a heart-felt reception, the greeting of the Westindian service personnel was distinctly low-key - possibly due to Britain being a country at war and having a war mentality firmly in grip of its psyche. Nowhere is the point made more conspicuously than in the responses made to the Westindian service personnel's request to be sent overseas. With the rebuttal statement that "you're already overseas," the view Britain had of the Westindian volunteers was apparent. The requester viewing themselves as being 'home,' while the respondent viewing the requester as a foreigner. Indeed, as many of the accounts from the service personnel reveal, the lifting of a veneer, as experience often does to pre-conception, disclosed a situation often imbued with prejudice and racism, elicited to a great extent by ignorance, ethnocentrism, intolerance and fear. As Robert Murray remarked:

"I never heard of racism until I got to Britain."

One of the striking impressions gained from the accounts is the different impacts the meeting of peoples from dissimilar, yet not totally alien, cultures was to have on each. WEB Dubois in "The Soul of Black Folk" has described this as "the problem of the twentieth century is the problem of the colour line - the relation of the darker to the lighter races of men." As one recalls, people from the Caribbean were seen as ideal for service in the British forces because of the compatibility between the cultures. While this meeting of peoples meant the shattering of a glorious illusion for most of the Westindians, it was the evoking of a ghoulish nightmare for the white British citizen, such were the discrepancies in stories each was told about the other. One cohort of people being fed an over-idealized and venerated portrait of Britain and its inhabitants, the other group being given a diet of stories which reduced people from outside Britain's shores to sub-human levels and hence produced a grotesque image of people from the colonies, especially the 'dark continents' as they were referred to. With hindsight, almost inevitably misunderstandings, apprehension, conflict and sheer hatred would abound. In this respect some white Britons were also victims of the colonization process, although to a lesser extent, as people from the Caribbean. The incident of the little boy who asked the black serviceman where his tail was, the response the boy gave when questioned about where he got such a concept from and his mother's response on hearing the black serviceman's reply to his concept, succinctly illustrates the situation - minds were colonized on both sides of the 'colour line'. Indeed, a conducive atmosphere existed for conflict and resentment, a situation which the authorities recognised by the development of "The Colonial Office," with its vague mandate to resolve some of these problems.

In order for some white British people to feel, or convince themselves, that they are in some way superior, an idea that had become embedded in their psyche, they must believe in an inferior 'other' group. Black people provided an easily distinguishable group to 'look down' on. While in an effort to discard these shackles, black people with hopes and aspirations would be challenging these long held views: - crossing over the 'colour line'. This point is further revealed by the fact that Westindians who had physical features that appeared white escaped much of the problems encountered by their black compatriots.

The violation of this colour line was made even more apparent in the eyes of white British individuals when mixed-race relationships started to occur. A prelude to the 'colour bar,' which essentially white males attempted to impose between black and white individuals, was blatantly revealed by the NCOs who accompanied the servicemen from their Caribbean paradise. The consorting of black men with white women was anathema to these white males as epitomized when the NCO opined: "no woman in England would consort with you." Beneath this comment lay the long held stereotype of black men being hypersexual; or, to quote Robert Staple, "beset by an unrestrained lustfulness." Therefore the sexual threat of energetic, healthy and young black men needed to be curtailed. Hence, the constant battles over women. It was quite paradoxical that for some Westindian ex-servicemen, one of the factors that induced them to enlist in the British Armed forces was Hitler's Super race theory; yet some of the behaviour, especially from white males to these ex-servicemen exhibited some of the worst ideas expounded in this theory.

The ex-World War veteran used in propaganda by the National Front conceives Westindians as an invading armada. This certainly was not the perception of those who set sail to Britain in the War years. The Westindian service personnel came to see but, unlike Caesar, they felt no need to conquer, for they had perceived Britain to be their home. However, fight they did, both in a literal and in a metaphorical sense, for what they wanted. Almost all the servicemen were to experience frustration, rejection and degradation at some time. The problems for black ex-servicemen in obtaining jobs and suitable accommodation, deeply unpleasant though this was at the time, did not and could not last forever. Some have fascinating stories to tell of life in civvy street, of hardship, of courage and of ultimate success.

It must be remembered that in those early days a great deal of prejudice emanated from fear and ignorance which could have had origins in the education system which sought to propagate and perpetuate such prejudice. The little boy who opined, "Mummy, mummy, it speaks!", and the farm-house girl who fled in a terrified state were both victims of a system that threatened young children with, "behave yourself or I'll call THE BLACK MAN!" One ventures to say that present-day children wouldn't bat an eyelid at such a threat; after all, such children might well be attending schools with black children or, at least, have regularly seen black cricketers, footballers, boxers and athletes on television. Many would conclude that the fights on RAF stations and outside referred to earlier in the book were dictated, to a certain extent, by a large concentration of numbers. Small numbers produced little or no trouble. Substantial numbers of Westindians, Americans, Welshmen or Scotsmen nearly always signalled violence. No fights ever occurred on stations where there were aircrew or servicewomen largely because of the paucity of numbers.

But there was another side to the experience of the Westindian service personnel during the War. As a few of the accounts convey, irrespective of the ex-service person's hue or persuasions, Britain was far from being a place consumed by gloom and doom as one might have expected with the menace of Nazism. Individuals never dwelt on the prospect of defeat. Some would say that a most happy-go-lucky atmosphere prevailed, particularly in the large cities. People lived from day to day, not knowing, or apparently caring, what tomorrow would bring. Laughter abounded everywhere. For the most part a spirit of *joie de vivre* predominated. One ex-serviceman vividly remembers a woman in Bristol deliberately sitting on an incendiary bomb and extricating herself to a safe distance just seconds before it exploded. This behaviour illustrates the 'devil-may-care' attitude that prevailed at the time. So fearless was she and so totally confident of coming to no harm that she displayed no visible signs of urgency.

In the streets, in the pubs, in the cinemas, in the dance-halls, in the parks, in a miscellany of places, the joys of life were seized and sucked dry. For the ex-servicemen, many would profess that life during the War was much preferred to that of today. People were said to be more affable, more altruistic and less materialistic. Robert Murray recalls, at times, "people going out of their way to help. Ask for directions and people would go miles to put you right."

The time eventually came when both jobs and accommodation needs were satisfied, more or less, and some of the ex-service personnel moved on to bigger and better things, forgetting the past. In the intervening years much water has flown under the bridge and, today, most of the ex-service personnel in the UK are happily settled and enjoying life. True, a small number of individuals indicate that they possibly could have enjoyed a better and more fruitful life had they not stayed in Britain and a few have drifted back to their homelands after retirement, but the vast majority remain.

In the meantime, let's consider the positive benefits resulting from the presence of black ex-servicemen and women in Britain - benefits for them, for their countries of origin and for the host country. They were the pioneers, the precursors to the large-scale settlement of blacks in the UK.

From the very early days those in the services benefited by always having money in their pockets. Even though three shillings (15p) a day was the 'norm' on joining up, there was enough to spare and still left something to send to grateful relatives. With hundreds sending money home, this had a beneficial effect on the economies of the countries concerned. In addition, those away in the forces were helping to solve the employment situation locally.

Many of the Westindian servicemen had a diversity of talents of their own, music, dancing, singing, weight-lifting, boxing, athletics and, of course, cricket, lovely cricket. One recalls Frank Holder from Guyana, a singer of considerable repute, performing with many leading bands of the day. Then, of course, there were those two splendid athletes, MacDonald-Bailey from Trinidad and Tobago and Arthur Wint from Jamaica. One remembers MacDonald-Bailey in Trinidad giving others handicaps of twenty and thirty yards and still beating them in a two hundred yards race. Both athletes took part in the 1948 Olympics at Wembley, MacDonald-Bailey running for England and Arthur Wint representing his native Jamaica. Wint, a man of extraordinary height, winning gold with consummate ease in the 440 yards with his legendary 11' stride, leading the field majestically, dwarfing the other runners as though they were midgets struggling to catch him. This undoubtedly brought fame and pleasure to the athlete as well as glory to his home country and host country, England.

When told the Flight Sergeant wouldn't release him, the Adjutant snapped: "Put him on." Immediately the Flight Sergeant turned from the telephone and ordered Robert Murray: "Drop everything and run!" Ever since that day the first question every morning was: "Any cricket today?"

Many of the servicemen were given training in a variety of trades in the RAF, like mechanics, engineering and driving and, although the majority seemed to have found difficulty in obtaining jobs in these trades immediately after the War, the situation gradually eased and they were able to apply their RAF skills which benefited them and the firms for which they worked; and Cy (Cyril) Grant, one of the early entertainers of radio and television with his melodious, Caribbean tunes, aided and abetted by his guitar, contributed by bringing untold pleasure to the thousands who listened and watched. In the end the host community gained as well.

To few of the benefits accruing to all sides already mentioned, there have been others - amongst them language. For generations, professors have been crossing the Atlantic as purveyors of English Language with Westindians the beneficiaries. As a result of the presence of WI ex-service personnel augmented by successive waves of immigrants, the situation has been reversed. Not only are Westindians teaching English in England but Patois has permeated the traditional language in poetry, literature and music. One readily calls to mind the calypso or reggae. In calypso, one recollects the first one to be almost universally accepted - 'CRICKET, LOVELY CRICKET,' commemorating the Westindies' first cricket Test Match victory in England in 1950, featuring the legendary Ramadhin and Valentine, sung with gusto by victors and vanquished alike. Not even the classics are now immune in this area. The steel bands have been very much to the fore and few classical pieces have escaped rendition by this means. Schools, particularly in the 'inner cities', and children of all races have taken to this novel form of music - taking to it like ducks taking to water. Some would consider it unthinkable to hold any prestigious function without the presence of a steel band and a number of the indigenous children are extremely adept at manipulating and effecting the most melodious sounds from the pans, something that would have been unheard of before World War II. Thus, another positive advantage has been gained by the host community from the presence of ex-service and immigrant Westindians.

In language, a native white girl has been overheard hurling obscenities at a black man in broad, broad Patois! And in inner city schools, children toss Patois phrases at each other like stones. And Westindian Art and Craft proliferate, particularly at Carnival time. Witness the intricate costume designs, the highly decorative floats and the miscellany of colours; in craft, the excellent basket-work and the articles made of clay and balatta (a juice from the balatta tree grown in Guyana).

Then there is food like rice and peas, curry goat, ackee and salt fish, pepper-pot, cassava, sweet potatoes, yams, plantains, green bananas and breadfruit - all have come to enrich the English cuisine; not forgetting the traditional Demerara, Barbadian and Jamaican sugar and rum; and herbal medicines like peppermint plant, lemon grass, pimento, Single-bible and Cerasee, suitable for many ailments including diabetes. Single-bible, also known as Aloe Vera, is widely used for a variety of complaints and ailments, such as burns, infection, wounds, constipation, liver diseases, insect bites, and even poisoning and dandruff; truly a panacea for ailments. All these herbal medicines are now seen as complementary to the traditional treatments provided within the health service.

Gone are the days when there used to be native complaints of smelly, spicy foods. They are all now simply known as foods, benefiting everyone. Here again, benefits accrue to all concerned, to those providing the services by way of foods, fruits, drinks, herbs or otherwise to the extent of the profits these generate. Then there are the exporting Caribbean Islands which gain, not only financially, but in the field of employment for their people there, not to mention their enhanced economies. Finally, to those in the UK who, perhaps for the first time in their lives, experience and enjoy entirely new brands of foods and cuisine, all made possible by those ex-service people from the Caribbean augmented by those who followed later as immigrants.

At the end of the War a large number of Westindian service personnel benefited by receiving courses as part of their rehabilitation and resettlement. These courses were awarded by the then Colonial Office primarily for the recipients, on qualifying, to return to their own countries to help in their post-War rebuilding. Many went back and did just that but a substantial number remained in the UK. Some felt that the courses were unfairly awarded, that many courses could have been longer and less intensive. But, as previously mentioned, courses were largely awarded on the basis of rank in the services. An officer stood a good chance of studying Law or Medicine as opposed to an 'Aircraft Hand General Duties' receiving a six-month course on, say, cabinet making.

However, whether the recipients returned to their homelands after training or stayed in the UK, there was no doubt that they benefited from the courses. Certain black professionals who stayed in the UK, such as doctors, chemists, chiropodists were quickly absorbed, while accountants, solicitors and most trades people found much initial difficulty. In the end, however, success came their way benefiting them as well as their employers and ultimately the host country.

Finally, one benefit that accrued to Westindian service personnel must be mentioned. This was known as the Scottish experience. Someone or some organization (generally assumed to be the British Council) felt it necessary to give Westindian service people an insight of life in Scotland, so that they could take this picture back to the Caribbean - it was generally assumed then, in 1945, that most, or all, in the services would be returning to their own countries. Many Westindians were selected to be given the experience which took the form of a 2-weeks full-time course at Glasgow University. Service people became university students for the period, living a similar life, receiving instructions by word and by vision on the geography, flora and fauna of Scotland in the mornings and then boarding coaches to tour various parts of the country, including sailing up the Lochs and a few rivers in the afternoons. To this day the ex-service personnel recall how beautiful Scotland was. It provided a wonderful experience for all those participating in it and had the very effect for which it was intended - some benefit indeed!

In contemplating the experiences of himself and other Westindian personnel, Robert Murray poses a question and attempts to supply an answer:

> " Why should anyone seek to remain in any country other than his or her own if he or she is unhappy? Why should he or she insist on staying if the indigenous population is constantly hostile? The answer, very few

would remain. The truth is that such has never been the case, not in any concerted manner anyway. The percentage of the indigenous population who would denigrate, abuse, and openly commit acts of violence against blacks, or anyone else for that matter, during wartime could only be described as minuscule and insignificant. It has often been said and, indeed, proved to be the case over the years, that the British, whatever their faults, are not a nation of extremes. Most would conclude, therefore, that they are not in general a belligerent people and that very few would embark on wholesale violence for no apparent reason. Some of those Westindians who were clamouring to be repatriated even before the War was over, and those who were perpetually vociferous about wanting to see the back of England, all now suddenly changed their minds, pleading to be allowed to stay. Even some of those who initially went back to their native lands after the War, returned to find their niche in the UK."

So, despite some of the examples of strife and, to a certain extent, unhappiness, portrayed in the previous pages, many benefits and advantages were gained by all concerned, from the presence of Westindian service and ex-service personnel in Britain.

The contribution of people from the Caribbean and other places to Britain's past and present position in the world community is seldom fully appreciated by the general public or, for that matter, by those in high political office. However, one of Britain's greatest statesmen didn't underplay this effort - Winston Churchill in 1956 stated:

"Our possession of the Westindies, like that of India ..... gave us the strength, the support, but especially the capital, the wealth, which enabled us to come through the great struggle of the Napoleonic Wars, and enabled us not only to acquire this worldwide appendage of possessions we have, but also lay the foundation of the commercial and financial leadership which, when the world was young, when everything outside Europe was undeveloped, enabled us to make our great position in the world."

Although Churchill's statement is resonant with a eurocentric and ethnocentric bias as indicated by the use of the term "undeveloped," he is fully cognisant of what we think of being BRITISH was born on the backs of its one-time colonies. As such the contribution of the Westindian ex-service personnel to the Napoleonic-like war effort now has been told. Moreover, to expand on an African theme, as long as those in the present remember the past then those people of the past will be animated and 'live on.'

EPILOGUE

A Light-Hearted Look at Getting Nearer Old Age

It's not hard to tell when you are getting old.
Everything hurts and what doesn't hurt doesn't work.
The Gleam in your eye is sun hitting your bi-focals.
You feel like the morning after, but you haven't been anywhere.
Your black book contains only names ending in MD.
You get winded playing cards.
Your children begin to look middle-aged.
You join a health club but don't go.
A dripping tap causes an uncontrollable urge.
You know all the answers but no one asks the questions.
You look forward to a dull evening.
You need glasses to find glasses.
You turn the light out for economy instead of romance.
You sit in a rocking chair but can't make it rock.
Your knees buckle but your belt won't.
Your back goes out more than you do.
You put your bra back to front and it fits better.
You sink your teeth in a steak and they stay there.
Your birthday cake collapses from the weight of the candles.
You just want to live long enough to be a problem to your kids.

Esther Armagon
(Jamaica)
Joined the ATC Branch of the RAF in 1944. After the war she became
a midwife.

190